Techniques of Twentieth Century Composition

BROWN

MUSIC SERIES

Consulting Editor

FREDERICK W. WESTPHAL,
Sacramento State College

BY THE SAME AUTHOR . . .

DALLIN: Listener's Guide to Musical
Understanding

DALLIN: Listener's Guide to Musical
Understanding Workbook

WINSLOW-DALLIN: Music Skills for Classroom Teachers

DALLIN: Foundations in Music Theory
(Wadsworth Publishing Company)

Techniques of Twentieth Century Composition

SECOND EDITION

Leon Dallin
California State College
Long Beach

WM. C. BROWN COMPANY PUBLISHERS
Dubuque, Iowa

Printed in the United States of America

To those who made this book possible
—my teachers, my students, my colleagues, and most especially my wife, who is the real writer in the family.

Preface to the Second Edition

The training of musicians no longer begins with the music of the eighteenth century and ends with that of the nineteenth century. Older and newer music deserve and are receiving added emphasis in college and university programs and in schools of music. This book is devoted to the music of the twentieth century.

Aspiring composers should begin to work with contemporary materials early in their creative careers. Performers must be prepared to cope with the intricacies of modern music. Teachers need to understand and appreciate it. All three categories are served by this text. It is designed to provide essential knowledge of twentieth century techniques and to bridge the gulf between traditional academic training and current practice.

Courses in traditional harmony and counterpoint are prescribed for prospective composers, performers, and teachers alike. The study of twentieth century music is a logical and necessary continuation. In conventional idioms technical proficiency and artistic discrimination are acquired, after familiarity through listening and playing, by analyzing and writing. The same procedures are effective for contemporary music. Applying them reveals the functional relationships between antiquated resources and their contemporary counterparts. Systematic utilization of new materials in creative exercises teaches composers to write the musical language of our time, performers to speak it, and listeners to understand it. The individuality of composers deliberately imitating established practices asserts itself in selecting from the infinite possibilities, but individuality is not something to strive for so much as something to emerge spontaneously with maturity and technical proficiency. Performers and teachers turn to their particular specialties before achieving this degree of attainment, but their musical insight is immeasurably enriched by temporarily assuming the role of composer.

Techniques of twentieth century composition are surveyed and illustrated. The examples, chosen on the basis of illustrating clearly the point under consideration, are drawn exclusively from the works of recognized composers. The coverage is comprehensive rather than selective. All important styles and procedures are included, but it is not suggested that every significant work and composer are represented. References to personal styles are incidental. The value of contemporary music as a whole is defended, but readers are encouraged to make their own evaluations of relative merit.

To facilitate the reading of the examples by less experienced musicians and to make them readily playable on the piano, only the treble and bass clefs are used. Orchestral scores have been reduced and transposed. Elements not essential to the problem have been omitted. Contemporary materials are related to conventional practices and are explained, as far as possible, in conventional terminology. The components of complex harmonies are arranged on the staff to reveal their underlying structures. New systems of analysis have been avoided.

The present volume evolved from efforts extending back to the 1940s to develop a logical and systematic presentation of the techniques and materials of twentieth century music to classes in composition and modern music. Teachers whose experience and training have been concentrated in the theoretical and traditional aspects of music rather than in the creative and contemporary, and composers who are more interested in creating new works than in organizing and systematizing their knowledge for the benefit of students should find it equally useful. I am indebted to the many students who tested and inspired the first edition. To these must be added the teachers whose comments contributed to the second edition and whose adoptions made it possible.

LD

Contents

Contents

Suggestions for the Use of This Book

The examples constitute a vital feature of this text. The sources are identified completely, and the dates of the composers and works are given in the *Index of Examples* at the back of the book. The excerpts should be studied carefully and played, either individually or in class. Part of the class time can be devoted profitably to discussion of the examples. Comments in the text are focused on the subject under consideration, but other aspects of the examples should not be ignored. Hearing recordings and studying the complete scores from which the examples are taken adds significantly to the understanding and appreciation of contemporary music as a whole and the specific passages in particular. The examples are most meaningful when seen in context and heard in the original medium.

The techniques and materials examined are in general use, and much is to be gained by searching out additional examples. Perceptive listeners and alert performers will strive continuously to identify and assimilate the twentieth century practices to which they are exposed.

It is not to be expected that the various types of modern music will be found equally attractive, but to make cogent evaluations and to produce mature compositions all must be familiar. It is preferable to explore every phase of contemporary composition, however briefly, than to concentrate on one to the exclusion of another. The relative amount of time spent in listening, analyzing, and writing will depend upon the objectives, interests, and abilities of the students.

Courses in composition and modern music are offered at different levels with varying prerequisites. These studies can be undertaken successfully with a minimal background of traditional harmony. Training in counterpoint, orchestration, and form is helpful but not essential.

In addition to doing specific assignments, students should be encouraged to do free creative writing in the style most natural for them at the moment. Compositions should be in forms and for mediums which are familiar and appealing. Even in the specified writing assignments the creative and expressive aspects should be emphasized. The concept should be one of sound rather than of abstract symbols. This manner of thinking is stimulated by writing for a particular instrument or ensemble with complete tempo, phrasing, dynamic, and articulation indications.

Whenever possible written exercises should be played with due regard for interpretation on the instrument(s) for which they are intended. For practical reasons much of the writing will be for piano which is both versatile and accessible. It is wise in the early stages to write for instruments one plays and with which one is familiar.

Students should see and hear each other's work and participate in discussions. Active participation motivates the class. Analysis of the mistakes and accomplishments of its members is informative and illuminating.

Sketchbooks of thematic ideas and files of creative exercises should be maintained as storehouses of raw material for future works. The muses are elusive and not always at the composer's beck and call.

A public performance is a stimulating experience for young composers. The full cycle of composition is achieved only when a work has been conceived, written, played, and heard. Through participation in the complete sequence composers become intimately aware of the practical problems of preparing and presenting their scores. This helps them to discover simple and effective ways of notating and developing their ideas. If the performance is recorded, they have the added advantage of repeated, undistracted hearings and opportunities to evaluate their scores objectively after the heat of creation has cooled. The value of such experiences cannot be rivaled by abstract instruction.

One final suggestion, and its validity is most certain, the only way to learn to compose is by composing.

CHAPTER 1

Introduction

Music majors in American colleges and universities generally receive excellent training in the theoretical aspects of music: harmony, solfege, counterpoint, orchestration, and form. These courses are considered an essential part of musical training. It is to be regretted that the study of composition does not universally follow, for only in composing are all of these techniques simultaneously employed for creative expression. Further, it is one of the best ways to develop that intangible but highly significant aspect of musical training, musicianship. Certainly those who have experienced the problems and pleasures of composing are better equipped both as teachers and performers. It is accepted as natural that all composers play. Should it not be just as natural for all players to compose?

Too often composition is regarded as a mystic art the practice of which is limited to a few great men of genius. A more realistic view is that the potential ability to compose is as widespread as the ability to play an instrument or sing. Few attain the stature of Beethoven and Bartok in composition, but how many attain the stature of Jascha Heifetz or Artur Rubinstein in performance? The answer to this question does not discourage thousands from starting the study of performance every year, and it should not discourage the embryonic composer. Certainly the urge to compose is as prevalent as the desire to play.

The study of composition has suffered from romantic emphasis on its inspirational elements and neglect of its technical aspects. The young composer is conditioned to think that inspiration cannot be taught or learned and should come therefore as readily to the novice as the master. Even if this were true, it would not eliminate the necessity for training

1

in composition any more than great talent eliminates the necessity for study and practice in performance.

The fact that everyone begins the study of music as a performer complicates the problem of teaching composition. Prior experience as performer and listener develops the ability to criticize and evaluate far beyond the ability to create. It requires patience on the part of the aspiring composer to develop his creative talents to the point where he is satisfied with his own efforts. During this developmental period, it is reassuring to realize that the works generally known of even the greatest composers come from their mature period and are not representative of their earliest efforts. Activities as a performer and listener are invaluable for the composer, but they do not automatically provide him with compositional skill.

A further complicating factor is the strong emphasis on the music of the romantic period in our musical conditioning. The musical idiom with which we are saturated is ill-suited to contemporary ideas. In this regard, the traditional theoretical training provides little direct help. However, if the study of theory has stressed the creative aspect of writing and the discipline has been based on broad, general principles rather than on rigid rules of a particular style, the transition can be made with a minimum of difficulty.

The importance of adequate training in conventional styles before free composition in contemporary idioms is not minimized. In spite of superficial evidence to the contrary, most twentieth century practices trace their roots back to the music of the past. Analyzed in terms of extensions of previous practices, many of the most complex passages in modern music become understandable and meaningful.

Suggested Assignments

1. Since knowledge of conventional materials and the ability to handle them effectively serves as a point of departure for the study of more recent idioms, demonstrate that ability by harmonizing the following folk song and chorale melody. Use a conventional style in four parts paying particular attention to the choice of harmony, balance of cadences, flow of harmonic changes, melodic value, spacing, and doubling.

Deficiencies in background will be apparent immediately in this familiar idiom, and they should be remedied before proceeding. The underlying principles involved are equally valid for all styles.

Ex. 1   The Ash Grove   *Folk Song*

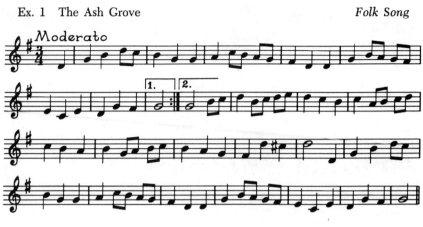

Ex. 2   Chorale   *Vulpius*

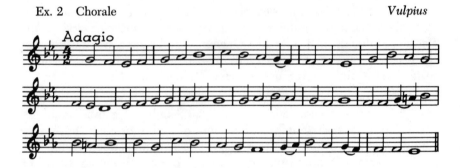

CHAPTER II

Melodic Contour and Organization

Of all the aspects of musical composition, the ability to write effective melodies is the most elusive, the most dependent upon natural gifts, and the most difficult to teach. But if one must rely upon natural gifts for the original conception of a melody, he can employ technique to put it in its most effective form and to make the best use of it.

Some composers seem to have been fortunate enough to conceive perfect melodies spontaneously. Mozart and Schubert apparently had this facility to a remarkable degree, but more often the original concept requires careful revision before it achieves maximum effectiveness. The sketchbooks of Beethoven provide ample proof of both the necessity and the value of such revision.

Example 3 shows various versions of the first eight measures of the second movement theme of Beethoven's *Third Symphony*. The first five versions, with certain alternate measures, appear in Beethoven's sketch book for 1803 as edited by Nottebohm.° The final version is the theme as it appears in the symphony. Beethoven wrote no key signature in the sketches, but the three flats appear to be intended throughout, corresponding with the final form.

A study of these sketches reveals the evolution of a commonplace germ idea, through various stages, into a classic melody. They also reveal how a master craftsman like Beethoven approached the problem of perfecting a crude original melodic thought. The lack of interest in the after phrase of the first version is corrected, and the dotted rhythm which occurs only once in the first version becomes a characteristic unifying factor in the later versions. Every feature of the completed melody ap-

---

°Breitkopf & Hartel, 1880.

pears in the sketches, but none is exactly like it. The finished product is a composite of the best elements arrived at progressively. There is but slight hint of strength and beauty in the original idea, but Beethoven had the technique and perseverance to realize its potential. These abilities are essential to the composer, for it is in this way many of the best melodies are produced.

Ex. 3   Sketches and Theme, Symphony No. 3 (2nd Mov't)   *Beethoven*

Unfortunately, the sketches of composers are not generally available, but much can be learned about their creative process as it affects melodic contour and organization through a study of the melodies in their works. Whether these melodies were created spontaneously or resulted from numerous revisions, they represent the version on which the composer put his final seal of approval. As such they provide models of structural and linear organization, and elements they have in common may well serve as criteria for evaluating and improving melodies of less mature composers.

The analysis is of necessity limited to features which can be observed objectively, though there exists in the best of them an elusive quality which defies analysis. A penetration of this mystery is not possible or necessary for the composer any more than a full knowledge of life is necessary for a doctor. It suffices for the composer to recognize the strengths and weaknesses of his ideas and to be able to develop the one and eliminate the other.

Characteristics of effective melodic writing may be observed in the following twentieth century melodies. The principles involved are equally apparent and valid in the music of previous periods, for contemporary practice is a continuation of tradition in matters of melodic contour and organization. Some twentieth century melodies demonstrate no new technical features, while others are expressed in terms distinctly peculiar to the period. The basic principles can be illustrated most clearly by examples drawn from the former. There is considerable variation in style, design, and length, but each presents a single idea ending with a more or less complete cadence. Single, complete musical ideas can be stated in a variety of ways, all of which are known generally as periods or sentences. Various typical period structures and contours are illustrated in the following examples.

Example 4 uses only the most conventional materials, diatonic notes of E major and equal divisions of the beat. Structurally, it provides a model for one of the most common patterns—one which abounds in folk music and is particularly appropriate for stating songlike melodies. The two halves of the melody begin similarly. The first ends with an incomplete cadence; the second with a complete cadence. The number of measures and the amount of repetition vary in this type of period. The basic elements are the similar beginnings of the two phrases and the incomplete and complete cadence implications.

Stepwise motion is predominant in the melody, and scale-line motion in the opposite direction invariably follows the descending fifths. There is a balance between the notes above and below the starting pitch. A climactic effect is lacking, because the highest note comes in both the first and third phrases. The scale line up from C-sharp in the eighth measure provides an effective bridge into the return of the opening. To fully appreciate the importance of this bridge, play the melody substituting a half note (like the other similar places) on C-sharp. Rhythmic motion at this point is essential to preserve the flow of the melody.

Ex. 4   The Firebird p18*   *Stravinsky*

Example 5 illustrates different features of structure and contour with equally conventional materials. The period consists of two contrasting phrases, a structure as common as that illustrated in Example 3. Interest is added by the extension of the after phrase effected by repeating the material of measure six in measure seven.

The low first note introduces a phrase leading to a climax point an octave higher at the semicadence. The climactic effect of this pitch is heightened by its duration and its repetition. Its significance is apparent though the pitch is exceeded by one step before the line begins its downward motion. In this typical contour ascending motion preceding the high point balances the descending motion following it. Two quarter notes on the first beat of the measure followed by descending motion to a note of longer value constitute the characteristic feature of the melody. This device occurs in five of the nine measures. In each instance, besides occurring on different pitches, it is subtly altered to avoid monotony while providing a strong unifying factor. The descending interval is successively a second, a fourth, a third, and finally a fifth. Only the fifth occurs more than once, and this is in connection with the extension. Since the melody is only part of a more extended composition, finality in the cadence is avoided by using the third of the scale instead of the tonic.

Ex. 5   The Wasps p23*   *Vaughan Williams*

By kind permission of J. Curwen & Sons, Ltd.

*Page numbers refer to the location of the excerpt in the source listed in the *Index of Examples.*

The contour of Example 6 might be considered an inversion of that in Example 5 since the middle of the melody is the low point with descending motion preceding and ascending following it. This is a concise statement of a telling melodic idea in a single five-measure phrase. Such short ideas frequently are repeated immediately, as this one is in the complete work. The repeated phrase has period function, and it represents another method of presenting a melodic idea. Unlike the period of Example 4, which it resembles, the cadences are the same for the statement and the repetition. Opportunities for internal repetition in a theme as brief as this are limited, but the two instances of dotted rhythm provide a unifying element, as does the recurrence at the end of the notes A, F-sharp, E from the beginning.

Ex. 6   Classical Symphony p20   *Prokofieff*

Of the preceding melodies, the contour of the Vaughan Williams with the high point in the middle is encountered much more frequently than that of the Prokofieff or the Stravinsky, but the most prevalent contour of all is illustrated in Example 7. Here the ascending motion of the first phrase culminates in a secondary high point, but the highest point and real climax is reached near the end of the melody following some preliminary descending motion at the beginning of the second phrase. This basic contour, in which a major portion of the melody is devoted to ascending motion and the climax comes toward the end, is typical of melodies in which the climax constitutes a predominant feature.

Example 7 is another period with contrasting phrases. The one-measure extension of the after phrase is achieved by delaying the resolution of the penultimate note. The treatment of the unifying devices is particularly interesting. The first five beats are repeated immediately, but interest is maintained by the rhythmic shift. Immediate repetition occurs similarly at the beginning of the after phrase. The repetition of this fragment corresponds rhythmically to the statement, but the substitution of eighth notes for quarters brings it to a different pitch. The eighth note neighboring tones of measures one and three are echoed in measure seven in a manner reminiscent of the usage of the dotted figure in Example 6. These neighboring tones also serve to stress the climactic effect of the E-flat in measure eight.

Ex. 7   Concerto for Violin No. 2 p3   *Prokofieff*

Still another contour and organization are illustrated in Example 8. The germ of this melody is contained in the motive which appears sequentially three times. A rapid ascent to the high point near the beginning is followed by a sequential descent to the cadence. This contour is not uncommon, but sequences of this sort are frowned on by many composers. Their excessive use rapidly becomes monotonous and causes stagnation in the melodic flow, but used in moderation and particularly when varied, they provide a strong unifying factor. Though the design of the motive is constant in this example, the quality of the arpeggio is different in each statement (major, diminished, minor) along with similar changes in the other intervals. Additional interest in melodies containing sequences is generally provided by the harmony and counterpoint associated with them.

This melody is only a phrase long, but it sounds perfectly complete in the slow tempo and with its strong cadence. Thematic interest is at a minimum in the last measure, and it serves little purpose other than to provide a close for the more telling motive of the opening.

Ex. 8   Symphony No. 2 p124   *Rachmaninoff*

In contrast to the previous example which made use of sequential repetition, the following shows immediate but varied repetition at the same pitch. In each instance the type of alteration is different. The repetition of the first section comes a beat later in the measure, and the end is altered to lead into the next section. The repetition of this section is

literal except for the melodic embellishment of the last two beats. The
characteristic rest on the beat of the third fragment is strikingly inter-
rupted in the repetition by the accented C-sharp in measure eleven, and
the process is reversed in measure twelve where the rest replaces the
accent. Each successive motive is shorter than its predecessor, and the
repetition is consistently abbreviated or embellished.

The internal structure, like that of many of the most interesting
melodies, does not conform to any traditional pattern. The high point
of the line comes near the middle, and, consistent with the character
of the melody, is repeated. The way each motive leads into the next with
an overlapping which makes it impossible to determine exactly where
one ends and the other begins must be ranked as a stroke of genius.

Ex. 9   Piano Sonatine p2   *Ravel*

Though a large percentage of melodies are cast in periods made
up of two phrases, any number of phrases may be used, and periods of
three and four phrases are common. Any presentation of a single, complete musical idea, regardless of the number of phrases it contains, is
functionally a period.

Example 10, which is a rather unusual group of five phrases and
quite unlike the previous examples in structure, illustrates the flexibility possible in phrase organization. It is unlike the previous examples
in still another way. Though it is the longest melody examined thus far,
it exploits the most meager resources. Few composers choose to limit

themselves to such drastic economy of means. The entire twenty measures, excepting only the cadence note, use only two rhythmic patterns within a measure, and four of the five phrases are rhythmically identical. Coupled with this is a strong similarity of line. When such economy is practiced, even the slightest variation assumes exaggerated importance, and Sibelius is careful to provide a token change in each phrase. Phrase 3 duplicates phrase 1 a third higher with resultant changes in the quality of the intervals. Phrase 4 stands in the same relation to phrase 2. The most notable deviation from the pattern and the one which does the most to rescue this melody from monotony, however, is the shift of the characteristic grace note and dotted rhythm from the third measure to the first of the concluding phrase.

Unusual economy of means and irregular form are coupled with the most ordinary contour. The high point comes toward the end of the melody in the fourth phrase, coinciding with the only dynamic indication.

Ex. 10   Pelleas and Melisande p5   *Sibelius*

For sheer number of notes involved, the theme of Ravel's *Bolero* must certainly rank as one of the most extensive melodies. For this reason it presents a particularly interesting example of musical organization. Divided in the middle by a comparatively strong semicadence, each half descends through a series of figures to the low C. The position of the high point in the middle is usual enough, but the approach to it is unique. It comes at the beginning of a phrase after a rest and is approached by leap instead of by the more usual gradual ascending motion.

Though the rhythmic subtlety of this melody can be appreciated fully only in association with its accompaniment, the skillful exploitation of rhythm is apparent, even isolated. The first impression is one of remarkable unity, but closer examination reveals a great diversity of detail. The only device which consistently recurs is that of the tie into the beat. This device appears twelve times, but even here the element of diversity is present. These twelve ties join seven different rhythmic combinations. Such ingenius manipulation of materials is evidence of technical skill.

Ex. 11   Bolero p1   *Ravel*

No discussion of melodic writing, even in the twentieth century, is complete without some mention of those emotion-packed melodies typical of the romantic era. For many people, this type of melody is almost synonymous with the word. Though no longer in vogue with the majority of composers, the ability to write such a tune is a priceless gift in any age. The difficulty of drawing with certainty the fine line between emotion and sentiment is perhaps one reason this aspect of the art is neglected now. The following example has become somewhat hackneyed through popular adaptions, but in the original it represents highly emotional writing at its finest.

With this type of melody particularly, an analysis of the external characteristics provides a minimum of insight. Its source and appeal are essentially subjective. The cadence points, though somewhat camouflaged, can be located, and the phrases, though unclearly delineated, can be isolated. The point of climax is effectively prepared, strategically located, and satisfactorily left. The lowered sixth degree of the scale, G-flat, (the key of the excerpt is B-flat) imparts a characteristic flavor to the melody. The sum of these features fails to account for the total effect. This stems rather from some impelling logic which defies analysis but which makes each note when heard in context sound inevitable. In creating a melody, this is a paramount virtue.

Ex. 12   Piano Concerto No. 2 p78   *Rachmaninoff*

The next three examples demonstrate slightly different applications of features disucussed in connection with the previous melodies. Number 13 is a group of three phrases. Observe the similarity of contour between Examples 5 and 15 and between Examples 11 and 14.

Ex. 13   Symphony No. 5 p65   *Shostakovich*

Ex. 14   Sonatine for Two Violins p8   *Milhaud*

Ex. 15   String Quartet No. 1 p5   *Thompson*

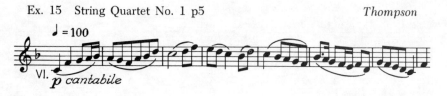

The foregoing examples provide a basis for some observations regarding desirable melodic characteristics. Perhaps no tune possesses all of them, and excellent melodies have features which are quite the opposite. This does not detract from the essential validity of these principles based on the practices of recognized composers. There is no formula for writing good melodies, but these models and suggestions will prove helpful in locating and correcting weaknesses, in evaluating results, and in putting creative efforts in their most effective form.

The very existence of twentieth century melodies using only the resources of earlier periods emphasizes the fact that contemporary techniques represent additions to and expansions of previous practices and not replacements for them. The concept of the creative artist as a perpetual innovator is without foundation. Firm contact with tradition should be maintained while exploring more recent trends.

Melodic ideas vary greatly in length. The idea itself determines what is appropriate. Longer melodies divide into phrases delineated by cadences. The location and distribution of these cadences are extremely important.

The cadence at the conclusion of an idea does not present a serious problem in melodies of definite tonality. They end on a note of the tonic harmony—root for the most conclusive, third and fifth for less conclusive closes. The cadential function must be clear, but trite formulas should be avoided. In cadences other than at the end of a work, the beginning of the next phrase should not be delayed too long, but the duration of the cadence note is not critical.

Incomplete cadences within a melody serve to pace the exposition of melodic ideas with a flow that is neither choppy nor aimless. The former results from cadence points too close together and too strong; the latter from cadence points too far apart and too weak. Semicadences most often are accomplished by momentary interruptions in the rhythmic flow. The proper duration for these interruptions is a subjective matter, but they should provide breathing places without causing loss of interest. Semicadences may occur on any pitch, and no one note should be overworked. Care should be exercised not to anticipate the finality of the complete cadence.

Modulation is possible but not essential. A melody may be entirely in one key; it may modulate or suggest a new key and then return (Example 12); or it may modulate and cadence in the new key (Examples 9 and 13).

Repetition is evident in most melodies. Coupled with a characteristic feature, which it often is, repetition provides a powerful unifying factor. For interest, repetitions are varied and embellished. Common types of modification include changes in intervals, pitch location, key, mode, rhythm, dynamics, and combinations of these.

A characteristic feature distinguishes most good melodies. No melody is unique in every detail, but some element must set it apart. The notable feature may be a rhythm, an interval, a motive, or anything which will serve as a means of identification.

In rhythm there should be balance between unity and variety. Notes of equal value and constant patterns lack rhythmic interest. Perpetual changes of duration and pattern reduce coherence. A limited number of patterns and values used with imagination is most effective.

Stepwise motion is basic in melodic writing, to which is added the spice of varied skips. Skips except along chord line are followed generally by a change of direction, often by step.

Melodic units with but one thought usually have a single focal point. This focal point, or climax, is most frequently associated with the highest pitch. The climactic effect can be enhanced by rhythmic prolongation, embellishments, and dynamics. A typical melodic line is concerned with approaching and leaving the focal point in the most effective manner. There is no formula for this, but it is of primary importance. The graphs of Examples 4 through 12, given in Example 16, show some typical melodic contours. The main climax usually is approached or followed by a series of lesser high points. A balance between ascending and descending motion is desirable, but the distribution must be determined subjectively. Too much emphasis on any one pitch is monotonous. This is especially true when the recurring note comes at cadences and at high, low, and turning points in the melody.

Ex. 16   Contour graphs of Examples 4 through 12

(a) Graph of Example 4

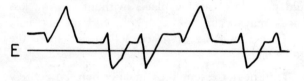

(b) Graph of Example 5

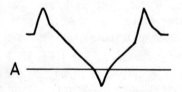

(c) Graph of Example 6

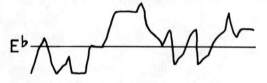

(d) Graph of Example 7

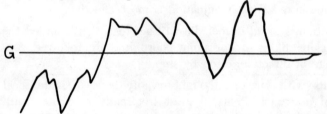

(e) Graph of Example 8

(f) Graph of Example 9

F#

(g) Graph of Example 10

F

F

(h) Graph of Example 11

C

(i) Graph of Example 12

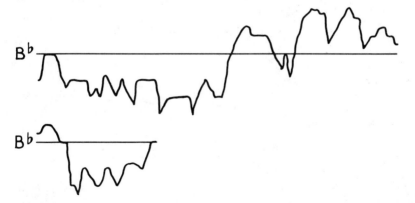

B♭

B♭

The foregoing comments summarize and the graphs illustrate characteristics of the examples and, indeed, of good melodies generally. It is admittedly easier to list the characteristics than to create melodies which embody them, because the quality of a melody is more dependent upon balance than upon the possession of specific features. Balance between unity and variety, activity and repose, ascending and descending motion, steps and skips, cadences, and climaxes is standard. The perception of balance is subjective, and subjective judgments are the product of taste. Impeccable taste is built on a foundation of keen instinct, thorough knowledge, and broad experience.

Suggested Assignments

1. Study Examples 13, 14, and 15 and list the most noteworthy features of contour, structure, and organization.

2. Analyze the melodic contour and organization of the themes from Prokofieff's *Classical Symphony, Opus 25*.

3. Locate other twentieth century melodies written in a traditional idiom, graph their contours, and discuss their distinctive characteristics.

4. Write original melodies using conventional materials. In the first ones follow the models rather closely in essential features of contour and organization. Later concentrate on developing strength of thematic idea and effectiveness of presentation in a more personal manner. After the melodies have been written, check them for compliance with the principles outlined in this chapter.

5. Make graphs of the original melodies written for Assignment 4. Examine the graphs for evidence of flaws and weaknesses in the melodic contours.

CHAPTER III

Modal
Melodic Resources

Contemporary composers have not been concerned exclusively with blazing unexplored trails. Many contemporary practices have resulted from the re-examination of earlier materials. Studies of plain chant, folk songs, and the vocal music of the sixteenth century, all of which make extensive use of the modes, have flourished in the present century. These studies have revived interest in the modes, neglected from Monteverdi to Debussy, as a source of musical materials. In the search for melodic resources beyond the arbitrary limitations of the major-minor system, they have proved to be a veritable gold mine.

The composer is not restricted to a traditional use of the modes but freely employs the extended resources of more varied scales. A knowledge of the modal music of previous periods is interesting and informative, but not absolutely essential for the exploitation of modal possibilities in a present-day idiom.

Ignoring their historical implications, the modes consist of a series of seven-tone scales with five whole tones and two semitones forming different patterns for each mode. All of the modes are produced by playing seven-note scales on the white keys of the piano starting on successive steps. The traditional designations for the modes are given in Example 17 with the location of the semitones marked for ready comparison.

Major and the natural minor scales form part of the modal system as the *Ionian* and *Aeolian* modes. The other modes are like one or the other of these with one scale degree altered, except the *Locrian* which has two. In Example 17 the notes which differ from major or minor are indicated with an arrow pointing in the direction of the deviation.

Ex. 17   The   Untransposed   Modes

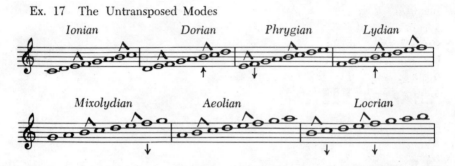

The arrangement of the whole steps and half steps in the modes is in every way just as natural as in major and minor, and the use of a mode as a source of material for a melody is just as valid. The modes are not to be considered as altered major or minor scales. However, ears saturated with major and minor music are apt to perceive them in terms of their deviation from the major-minor patterns, and this deviation then asserts itself as the distinctive feature of the mode. In preliminary work with the modes it is useful to keep this feature in mind and to exploit it consciously. The following table showing the deviation of each mode from major or natural minor is given for reference.

Ionian. . . . . . . like major
Dorian. . . . . . like minor with the sixth degree raised
Phrygian. . . . . like minor with the second degree lowered
Lydian. . . . . . like major with the fourth degree raised
Mixolydian. . . . like major with the seventh degree lowered
Aeolian . . . . . like minor
Locrian. . . . . . like minor with the second and fifth degrees lowered

It is emphasized that the modes were not derived from the major and minor scales, but students trained in traditional harmony usually find this association and the association of the untransposed modes with the white keys of the piano the easiest ways to recognize and remember them.

A distinction must be maintained between the characteristic notes of the modes and the occurrence of these same relationships as chromatic tones in tonal (i. e., major or minor) melodies. As chromatic notes they have an auxiliary function and a decided tendency to resolve in the direction of the alteration. By contrast, their function in the modes is basic, and they are free to progress either up or down by step or skip. They behave exactly like diatonic notes which, in the modes, they actually are.

All of the modes may be transposed to any scale degree by using the proper signature or accidentals in the same manner as major and minor are transposed. The proper signature for a mode can be worked out by determining what flats or sharps are necessary to produce half steps in the desired positions. A formula can be derived by thinking of the relationship of the untransposed mode to C major. For example, the Dorian mode is like a major scale beginning on its second degree, or stated another way, the Dorian mode has the same signature as the major scale a major second below. Thus, the Dorian mode on G would have the same signature as the major scale a tone below, which is F with one flat. The Phrygian mode has the same signature as the major scale a major third below, so Phrygian on C-sharp would have the same signature as A major or three sharps. This process can be continued to determine the signature for any mode on any pitch. The fact that a mode has the same signature as some major scale must not be construed to constitute a relationship between them.

Essentially this same process will serve to determine the mode when the tonic and the signature are known. For example, if the tonic (the *final* in modal terminology) is A and the signature is four sharps, the mode would be Lydian since the signature is that of the major scale a perfect fourth below.

There is no uniform practice in the use of signatures for modal music. Some composers use the signature which produces the mode without the use of accidentals. Others use the major or minor signature which is closest to that of the mode and then add the necessary accidentals. This practice is usual when only part of the composition is modal. In many recent works there are no signatures, and accidentals are used as required. This practice has the same advantages and disadvantages in modal as in tonal writing. When there are frequent shifts in the key center, it avoids the problem of excessive cancellations, but sharps and flats must be indicated each time they occur.

The following melodies from the works of twentieth century composers are written in a mode or show modal influence. It is entirely within the realm of possibility that the modal influences were sometimes subconscious and that the composers were not using specific modal materials by design. The perception of the tonal center is somewhat subjective, so there are times when the tonal center and consequently the mode are open to more than one interpretation. In some cases, too, the accompanying materials suggest a center different from that of the mel-‘ody. These facts, however, do not detract from the genuineness of the modal influences or from their contribution to melodic resources.

Example 18 is Roy Harris' version of the familiar folk song *Wayfaring Stranger*. The signature is six flats, but the consistent cancellation of the flats on C and G produces a Dorian mode on B-flat.

Ex. 18   American Ballads No. 2   *Harris*

There are no sharps or flats in the signature of Example 19, but F-sharp is used consistently. The cadences are alternately on C and A. A scale on C with F-sharp would be Lydian, but Dorian on A emerges as the mode of this example and the movement from which it is taken.

Ex. 19   Piano Sonatina p5   *Bartok*

A more extended melody in D Dorian is given in Example 20. G-sharp occurs five times as a chromatic neighboring tone, but in each instance it resolves as such without disrupting the feeling for the mode. In contrast, the B-natural which is diatonic in the mode, though raised from the signature, more often than not resolves downward. The B-flat near the end of the melody suggests a change to the Aeolian mode, and the final E-flat results in a modulation.

Ex. 20   Violin Concerto p3   *Sibelius*

The Phrygian mode with its center on G is illustrated in Example 21.

Ex. 21   Fantasia on a Theme by Tallis p6   *Vaughan Williams*

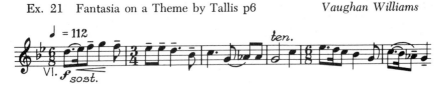

The setting for Example 22 suggests D minor, but the melody considered by itself is a particularly clear and beautiful example of Phrygian on A.

Ex. 22   String Quartet p5   *Ravel*

Randall Thompson uses the Phrygian mode with the tonic on G in the following melody from his string quartet.

Ex. 23   String Quartet No. 1 p12   *Thompson*

The interval of the augmented fourth has thematic significance in the Sibelius *Fourth Symphony.* When this interval comes between the keynote and the fourth degree of the scale, as it does in Example 24, the Lydian mode is suggested. The B-natural can be considered as a chromatic lower neighbor to the C, but its thematic use elsewhere in the work lends weight to the modal concept.

Ex. 24   Symphony No. 4 p14   *Sibelius*

Allegro molto vivace

The distinction between major and Lydian is not always clear because of the frequent use of sharp four of the scale in major. Also, the use of the augmented fourth above the tonic, the characteristic note of the Lydian mode, tends to create the impression of a modulation. This is the case in Example 25, though the extensive use of modes throughout the work supports the modal analysis of this passage when it is in context.

Ex. 25   Concerto Gregoriano p18   *Respighi*

F-sharp as a chromatic tone in C major has a definite tendency to resolve upward. Since, in Example 26, the line continues down after the F-sharp, the Lydian influence is emphasized even though the next fragment suggests C major.

Ex. 26   Symphony No. 2 (Romantic) p32   *Hanson*

The feature of the major scale which composers find most restricting is the tendency of the leading tone to resolve up to the tonic. This tendency is so strong that in many progressions no other voice leading is satisfactory. For this reason melodic lines and harmonic progressions involving the leading tone have been the most subject to stereotyping. Finding an effective substitute for the clichés involving the leading tone is one of the most perplexing problems for composers breaking away from traditional formulas. One solution is to avoid the leading tone, and this is provided by the Mixolydian mode which otherwise has all the characteristics of major. This accounts for the frequency with which Mixolydian is used and perhaps for the excellence of extended melodies conceived entirely in it. The next three examples are representative.

Except for the rapid run leading to the octave transposition in the afterphrase, in which the notes can scarcely be distinguished, Example 27 is in the Mixolydian mode on D. The signature does not indicate the mode, but the necessary sharps and naturals are applied regularly.

Ex. 27   The Wasps p8   *Vaughan Williams*

The *Prologue* in Britten's *Serenade* is written for unaccompanied French Horn. Given in its entirety in Example 28, it is in the Mixolydian mode on F throughout.

Ex. 28   Serenade: Prologue p1   *Britten*

Example 29 is another extended melody in pure Mixolydian, this one untransposed on G.

Ex. 29   Violin Sonata p17   *Copland*

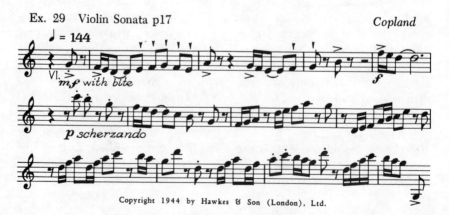

So much emphasis is placed on the melodic and harmonic forms of minor in the study of harmony, the natural minor or Aeolian constitutes virtually a new sound for many, even though it exists in traditional theory. For this reason examples are given. Examples 30 and 31 are untransposed Aeolian, and Example 32 is Aeolian on D. All three use only the notes of the pure mode.

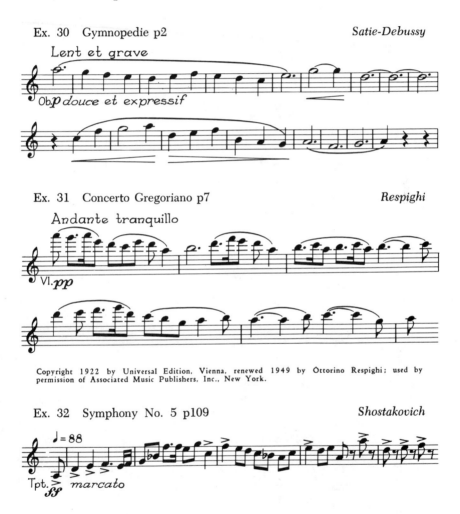

Ex. 30   Gymnopedie p2   *Satie-Debussy*

Ex. 31   Concerto Gregoriano p7   *Respighi*

Copyright 1922 by Universal Edition, Vienna, renewed 1949 by Ottorino Respighi; used by permission of Associated Music Publishers, Inc., New York.

Ex. 32   Symphony No. 5 p109   *Shostakovich*

The Locrian mode is rarely encountered in the music of any period. Some theorists, while admitting its existence in theory, deny its use in actual practice. The next three melodies, however, appear to be Locrian. Example 33 is untransposed on B. Only one chromatic passing tone is out of the mode, and it has all the notes of the mode except A. There is some use of F-sharp in the accompaniment which would make the mode Phrygian, but the cadence chord is a Locrian tonic seventh.

Ex. 33   Violin Concerto p24   *Khatchaturian*

The composer designates C the tonic in Example 34. After the first note, all are in the Locrian mode and only the third is missing.

Ex. 34   Ludus Tonalis: Fuga Prima in C   *Hindemith*

Isolated, the melodic fragment in Example 35 could be either Phrygian on G or Locrian on D, but the latter is confirmed as the tonic.

Ex. 35   A Ceremony of Carols No. 8   *Britten*

Academic distinctions are sometimes made between Ionian and major, but for purposes of composition and analysis they are identical.

Since all of the examples in major of Chapter II may be regarded also as Ionian, none are given here.

The specific characteristics of each mode are essential to well conceived modal melodies. This can be demonstrated impressively by playing the foregoing examples substituting notes of the major or minor scale for the distinctive notes of the modes. Some of the most effective of the melodies are thereby reduced to the most ordinary. This again points up the fallacy of regarding the modes as corruptions of the more familiar scales.

The adoption of the modes puts at the disposal of the composers not only the characteristic tones of the individual modes, but when considered collectively, makes accessible all of the notes of the chromatic scale as diatonic material. This is demonstrated by building all of the modes on C.

Ex. 36   The modes on C

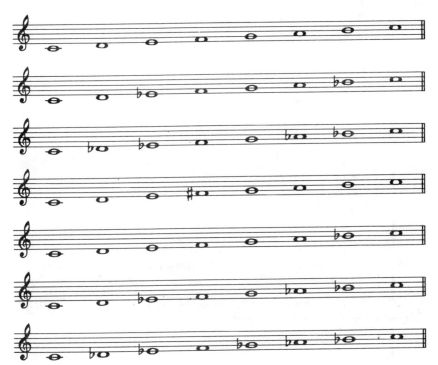

A composite of Example 36 shows the modes on C in which the various notes of the chromatic scale occur.

Ex. 37   Composite of Modes with C Tonic

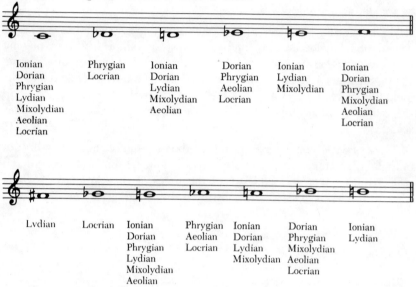

Ionian	Phrygian	Ionian	Dorian	Ionian	Ionian
Dorian	Locrian	Dorian	Phrygian	Lydian	Dorian
Phrygian		Lydian	Aeolian	Mixolydian	Phrygian
Lydian		Mixolydian	Locrian		Mixolydian
Mixolydian		Aeolian			Aeolian
Aeolian					Locrian
Locrian					

Lydian	Locrian	Ionian	Phrygian	Ionian	Dorian	Ionian
		Dorian	Aeolian	Dorian	Phrygian	Lydian
		Phrygian	Locrian	Lydian	Mixolydian	
		Lydian		Mixolydian	Aeolian	
		Mixolydian			Locrian	
		Aeolian				

Since the modes have much in common with major and minor and are a definite part of our musical heritage, yet contain vastly expanded resources, they offer an ideal point of departure from tradition.

Suggested Assignments

1. Write the proper signature for the following modes:
   a. Dorian on E.
   b. Aeolian on F.
   c. Lydian on B-flat.

2. Name the mode when:
   a. The signature is two sharps and the tonal center is A.
   b. The signature is four flats and the tonal center is C.
   c. The signature is one sharp and the tonal center is F-sharp.

3. Determine the tonal center and mode of the themes in Ravel's *String Quartet in F major*. Note changes in recurrences of the themes.

4. Locate additional twentieth century melodies which exhibit modal influences.

5. Write original melodies in each of the modes. At first use pure modes with a definite tonal center and exploit the characteristic features. Later apply modal concepts freely in spontaneous melodic invention.

CHAPTER IV

Distinctive Twentieth Century Melodic Practices

The free transposition of either the major-minor or modal systems requires the use of all twelve tones accommodated by our present instruments and notation. All of these sounds became practical with the adoption of equal temperament over two hundred years ago, but new ways of combining them still are being found.

Until recently the accepted practice was to use selective scales of seven notes arranged in a few stereotyped patterns as basic material within a key, and to admit the other five notes incidentally in secondary roles. Current practice is to exploit more fully the potential variety inherent in the twelve available sounds through greater freedom in the formation of scale patterns, in linear organization, and in tonality. This chapter is concerned with some of the specific ways this new-found freedom has been employed in melodies of the present century.

The exercise of these freedoms is not a universal feature of contemporary melodic writing. While their use may be regarded as characteristic, many recent melodies are in styles not foreign to previous periods. New practices have been added to the old, but the old have not disappeared. The features which distinguish the melodic writing of the present are not clearly delineated and used independently, but for purposes of study it simplifies the problem to consider them individually.

Nonvocal Melodic Lines

Vocal influences permeate the melodies of the classic and romantic periods, even in instrumental works. Singable melodies are the norm for these periods, and singableness is still cited on occasion as a measure of melodic value. This test is less applicable to the music of the baroque era and has very little validity for the music of the present. While many melodies of our time can be sung with ease, other equally good melodies are decidedly nonvocal and unsingable.

Nonvocal characteristics are manifest in various ways. One is the use of extended range. In view of the practical ranges of orchestral and keyboard instruments, it is remarkable that so many melodies written for them observe the limitations of the voice. Examples 38, 39, and 40 explore the extended ranges of the instruments for which they are written.

The essential lyric quality of the violin and of many vocal melodies is preserved in Example 38 while covering a range in excess of two octaves within three measures.

Ex. 38   Violin Concerto No. 2 p5   *Prokofieff*

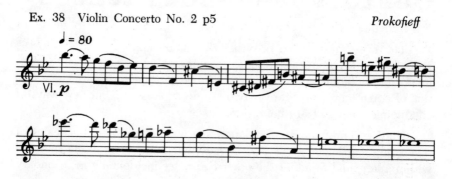

Example 39 ranges over the keyboard with typical octave transpositions and leaps. No small part of the effectiveness of this melody is due to the changes of register, as playing it with the parts all transposed to the same octave will demonstrate.

Ex. 39   Piano Sonata p3   *Copland*

From the same work as Example 39, Example 40 shows another procedure leading to extended melodic range. Here the extended range is the result of leaps continuing in the same direction instead of reversing in the conventional manner.

Ex. 40   Piano Sonata p19   *Copland*

Sometimes the extended range results from what appears to be an octave transposition of segments of the melody, even though no octave leaps are used. Example 41 (a) is a melody of this type, and Example 41 (b) shows it reduced to conventional range and leaps.

Ex. 41(a)   Violin Concerto No. 2 p8   *Milhaud*

Ex. 41(b)   The above reduced to conventional range

It is not presumed that composers conceive melodies with conventional compasses and then transpose segments of them, but this type of analysis demonstrates an affinity between conventional melodic contours and some contemporary melodies which otherwise might not be apparent.

When the segments occurring in different octaves are reduced to one or two notes, the result is an angular melody with a minimum of vocal influence. In Example 42 the interval of a ninth, which can be

analyzed as a second transposed an octave, constitutes the characteristic feature and accounts for its pronounced angularity.

Ex. 42   Symphony No. 5 p61   *Prokofieff*

Example 43 illustrates the ultimate in change of octave with alternate
notes in different octaves. The consistent alternation of registers almost
leads to the perception of two melodic streams, one in the upper octave,
the other in the lower, though this effect is minimized by the short duration of the lower notes. Transposed up an octave, the thirty-second notes
would be merely chromatic neighboring tones.

Ex. 43   Three Piano Pieces Op. 11 No. 1   *Schoenberg*

Some melodies written for voice are the least vocal in style by conventional standards. Example 44, though written for soprano voice, demonstrates many of the nonvocal characteristics previously discussed. It
has wide and unusual intervals and a compass in excess of two octaves.
The realization of such a melody in performance presents problems of
extreme difficulty, so this degree of complexity is not recommended for
composers who must rely upon amateur singers for performance. It
illustrates how the concept of melodic line has broadened in recent times,
and its performance demonstrates vocal capabilities unsuspected a few
decades ago.

Ex. 44   Wozzeck p87   *Berg*

Additional Scale Resources

The scale resources considered thus far have been limited to those consisting of seven notes comprising five tones and two semitones. Though these scale patterns have dominated European music for several centuries, there is no justification for limiting melodic resources to them exclusively. Other patterns long have been favored by non-European cultures, and recent tendencies in Western music have been in the direction of exploiting additional scale resources.

An interesting study can be made of the origin and development of the various scale materials, but this is not the primary province of the composer. His concern is the application of these materials.

One of the most ancient scales is the pentatonic, with five notes in the relationship of the black keys of the piano. Example 45 is a passage from Debussy using these specific notes.

Ex. 45   Nocturnes: 1.   Nuages p12   *Debussy*

In the pentatonic scale, each note may serve as a tonic, and any note which is stressed or on which a cadence occurs will tend to assert itself as such. The scale pattern shown is the most time-honored. In this particular example the tonal center seems to shift from F-sharp to G-sharp, but persons conditioned in the major-minor system do not have a strong feeling for the tonal center in pentatonic music in any event.

A conscious use of the pentatonic scale is indicated in the Ravel quartet where these two melodies appear in juxtaposition.

Ex. 46   String Quartet in F major p37   *Ravel*

Ex. 47   String Quartet in F major p38   *Ravel*

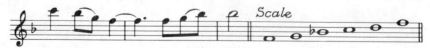

The melody in Example 47, from the last movement, is a cyclic re-iteration of a first movement theme originally stated in the Phrygian mode. (See Example 22.) The scale for this example is given in the same pattern as that of the previous examples, but the cadence at the end suggests B-flat as the tonic after earlier emphasis on C.

The pentatonic scale is not used now for entire compositions, ex-cepting possibly for program music with an oriental flavor, but it is effective for short passages as these excerpts show.

Five-note scales are possible in patterns other than that of the an-cient pentatonic. Example 48 is a melody of Stravinsky using five notes in a different spacing.

Ex. 48   The Rite of Spring p17   *Stravinsky*

Motives with few notes and a limited compass abound in the music of Stravinsky, but they do not often suggest a scale pattern as clearly as this because of their brevity. The five notes of this scale could come from either the Dorian or Aeolian modes with G as the tonic.

Example 49 shows a pronounced influence of the Phrygian mode, but since the fourth degree of the scale is not present, all of the notes of the melody come from two similar three note patterns a major third apart.

Ex. 49   String Quartet p1   *Debussy*

A six-tone scale more often associated with Debussy is the whole tone scale. Since the potential of this scale is extremely limited both harmonically and melodically, it does not figure as prominently in impressionist music as some are inclined to think. Only two whole tone scales are possible, starting on adjacent half steps, and the harmonies contain only major seconds and major thirds in various combinations and inversions. These inherent limitations make the whole tone scale more useful in isolated coloristic passages and in conjunction with other materials than as an exclusive basis for extended works.

The tendency of young composers, once they have discovered the whole tone scale, is frequently to use it to excess. Example 50 shows an isolated use of it by Debussy. A study of some complete works will reveal how he integrates it in his total technique.

Ex. 50   Preludes Book 1   No. 2   *Debussy*

The short, descriptive *Prelude* from which Example 50 is taken is based melodically and harmonically on this one whole tone scale except for a brief passage in the middle. The complete piece will interest those attracted to this technique. Observe the enharmonic spellings.

The absence of a leading tone and the uniformity of all scale intervals cause the feeling for tonality to be vague, if not nonexistent, in music written entirely in whole tones.

Example 51 shows an incidental whole tone influence in a strongly tonal work. F is the tonic throughout the melody, and the after phrase is F major. The whole tones seem to be derived from a combination of the first three notes of the ascending F major scale with the first three notes of the descending F minor scale. This results in a mirroring of the intervals, the two whole steps above F being mirrored by the two whole steps below.

Ex. 51   The Wasps p4   *Vaughan Williams*

Mirroring of scale degrees is carried further in Example 52 by Bartok. In the most conventional terms, the scale on which it is based is made up of the lower tetrachord of a major scale and the upper tetrachord of a natural or descending melodic minor scale. The scale material also may be analyzed as a mirroring of the first five notes of the major scale, with a tone-tone-semitone pattern both up and down from E. This analysis is supported by the mirror imitation between the two hands.

Ex. 52   Mikrokosmos Vol. 1 No. 29   *Bartok*

Whatever its derivation this scale affords note combinations not available in major, minor, or any mode. Infinite variety is possible in constructing scales of this sort. For lack of a better and generally accepted designation, such scales will be called *synthetic scales*. Synthetic scales represent a fruitful source of contemporary materials which is far from exhausted.

Bela Bartok is particularly ingenious in the derivation and use of synthetic scales. Some of his unconventional scale materials seem to be purely contrived while others stem from non-Western musical traditions. Synthetic scale structures underlie several pieces in his *Mikrokosmos*. Because of their simplicity they provide an excellent introduction to this device.

In Example 53 unconventional signatures, different in each hand, produce a synthetic scale. Only those notes shown on the top staff and their octaves are played by the right hand, and only those shown on the bottom staff and their octaves are played by the left hand. C is the tonic. With the notes arranged as they are on the example and as they occur in the piece, the mirroring of the intervals is apparent. Unlike the previous examples, however, the mirroring does not start from the same pitch.

Ex. 53   Scale of Mikrokosmos Vol. III No. 99   *Bartok*

The tonic in Example 54 is G with a signature of one sharp on C. This scale combines elements of two modes—the augmented fourth of Lydian with the minor seventh of Mixolydian.

Ex. 54   Scale of Mikrokosmos Vol. 11 No. 41   *Bartok*

No signature is used in the source of Example 55. The scale is made up of two major pentachords a diminished fifth apart. This extends the compass beyond an octave, which is possible in synthetic scales if different inflections of notes are used in the second octave. It also is possible to use different inflections in the same octave like the C-natural and C-sharp.

Ex. 55   Scale of Mikrokosmos Vol. III No. 86   *Bartok*

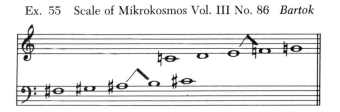

Since each pentachord appears in a different hand, this piece could be perceived as being in two keys simultaneously. Consideration of this possibility is delayed until Chapter VIII.

Example 56 shows a synthetic scale resulting from the combination of two signatures. The signatures themselves are not as unconventional as they appear. The E-flat and A-flat which normally precede D-flat in the signature could as well be added to the top part, but they would be meaningless since those notes do not occur. One sharp on F is the usual signature, but it appears unusual when placed in the bottom space instead of on the top line. Bartok places the sharp where it occurs in the melody rather than in the conventional place, but the effect is the same.

Ex. 56.   44 Violin Duets Vol. 1 No. 11   *Bartok*

E is the tonal center of Example 56. It begins on E and ends with the diminished fifth E and B-flat. The scale consists of alternating whole and half steps up from the tonic. Placing the D-natural below the tonic, an eight-note scale from D-natural to D-flat with the second note as tonic results. The practice of placing the tonic other than at the bottom of the scale has historical precedent in the plagal forms of the modes.

Unconventional key signatures are an added hazard for the performer, who has to ignore years of conditioning in the conventional arrangements of the flats and sharps when they are used. The association of the flats and sharps with a certain position and order is not abandoned easily. Unusual placements and the use of more than one signature are effective ways of devising new scales, and their use in scores is not too disturbing. It is generally inadvisable to use them in parts, piano, and vocal music. This is particularly true for orchestral parts when rehearsal time is limited. Preferable procedures are to use no signature or the conventional signature which most closely approximates the synthetic scale, adding accidentals and cancellations as required. The result is the same, and maximum efficiency in learning the work and performing it accurately are assured.

Benjamin Britten uses a conventional signature in Example 57, which is based on a synthetic scale. The tonic is G, and he uses the signature of G minor. A-flat is used consistently, and it could be added to the signature without violating the normal order or arrangement of the flats. However, he chooses to indicate it each time with an accidental. The C-sharp and D-flat are used as chromatic neighboring tones. Omitting these, the scale is like harmonic minor with a flat second degree or like the Phrygian mode with a sharp seventh degree.

Ex. 57   Serenade: Dirge p18   *Britten*

In Example 58, Griffes follows the same practice as Britten, using the signature of B minor for the melody with B as its tonal center. The scale, with its two augmented seconds, is synthetic as far as the major-minor and modal systems are concerned, but it does occur in our music with sufficient frequency to have a common designation—that of *gypsy scale*. Though not part of the basic scale system of the music of Western Europe, it is used extensively in other parts of the world. It serves well to evoke the oriental atmosphere of the Coleridge poem on which the music is based.

Ex. 58   The Pleasure Dome of Kubla Khan p 16   *Griffes*

This consideration of additional scale resources is by no means exhaustive. It merely indicates some of the new patterns that have been used and hints at the manner in which they may have been conceived. These examples point the way for unlimited development in the basic process of scale invention. This technique is valuable, because music based on a selective scale, even a synthetic one, is generally more homogeneous than music lacking such a foundation.

Expanded Tonality

Limitations imposed by rigid, selective scale concepts have diminished continuously during the course of Western music history. By the end of the romantic era chromatic tones were employed to such an extent they rivaled the tones of the scale in importance and frequency of use though selective scales and tonality had not been abandoned. Increased chromaticism coupled with free and frequent modulation led to a greatly expanded tonality. Carried to its logical conclusion, chromaticism leads to an all-inclusive scale of twelve notes with equal status known as a *duodecuple* scale. This designation is more precise than chromatic scale even though the notes are the same, because it does not carry with it connotations of altered or secondary tones. The duodecuple scale provides maximum freedom in melodic construction, but the unifying force of selective scales and tonality are lost in the bargain. This poses a problem that has been attacked by contemporary composers in three basic ways.

The first is simply to deny the importance of tonality—to renounce it as a desirable quality. Music with no tonal center is called *atonal.*

Such music enjoys the advantages of absolute freedom but risks being unintelligible. Uninitiated listeners find atonal music difficult to comprehend and appreciate.

Atonality is by nature a negative quality, but even so it is not easily achieved. Any note which recurs more than the others, appears in strategic or cadential points, or is stressed in any way tends to assert itself as a tonic. Atonality is not something which occurs spontaneously but something which must be cultivated consciously, and achieving atonality is no guarantee of quality. Atonal melodies must have merit in spite of their lack of tonality, for it does not follow automatically that they will have merit because of it. Avoiding tonality and at the same time attaining desirable melodic traits taxes the skill of experienced composers. For this reason the cultivation of free (i.e., nonserial) atonality by novices is not encouraged. If it occurs spontaneously, there is no objection to it.

The vanishing point of tonality is not easily pinpointed. In the final analysis it is a subjective matter. Almost any combination of tones suggests a tonal center to some musicians while definite tonal relations must exist before tonality is perceived by others. The former would detect evidence of a tonal center, perhaps F, in Example 44, but the latter would probably regard it as atonal.

Example 59 approaches atonality, yet it is basically simple. This sort of melody, though lacking strong tonal orientation, has no insurmountable obstacles to comprehension. The movement of the melody along familiar triad lines provides a bond with tradition and previous experience.

Ex. 59   Wozzeck p45   *Berg*

Music in which tonality is renounced without any substitutes being provided is rare in the twentieth century. Atonal music of our time more often uses a *note series* or *tone row* which provides both a systematic way of achieving atonality and a unifying element to take the place of tonality. The *twelve-tone technique* or *tone-row technique,* as it is commonly called, is the second basic way in which composers have attempted to organize twentieth century materials. This approach is so unique and represents such a break with tradition, it is considered separately in Chapter XIV.

The third approach, though it has no specific designation, is abundantly represented in contemporary works. They have definite tonal centers and reaffirm the significance of tonality. The concept of tonality, however, differs from that of previous periods. No hierarchy among the twelve tones is recognized with the single exception of the tonic. The tonic retains its traditional function, but the other eleven tones are equal, free, and independent of each other. This concept will be called *free tonality.*

There is no clear line of demarcation between free tonality and late nineteenth century ultrachromaticism. Example 60 might be considered a borderline case. In this example all twelve notes are used with no great preference being shown for those that belong to the key, F minor. Statistically there are eighteen occurrences of the five notes out of the key and twenty-nine occurrences of the seven notes in the key. The proportions approximate those anticipated with the complete acceptance of the free tonality concept. On the other hand, a large percentage of the notes out of the key are chromatic passing tones. Only the G-flats of measures 1 and 5 and the E-naturals of measures 4 and 7 do not resolve by half step. Even these eventually arrive at their normal resolution, the G-flat with one note intervening, the E-natural with seven. The voice leading is more representative of the nineteenth century than of the twentieth.

Ex. 60   Symphony No. 1 p4   *Shostakovich*

A more typical use of free tonality is evident in Example 61. The tonal center of F-sharp is established by the ascending fourth at the beginning and the clear cadence on that note at the end. In between, all twelve notes are used with equal freedom and independence. The conventional tendency for notes to resolve in the direction of their alteration is noticeably absent. This is to be expected, since in free tonality and the duodecuple scale there are, strictly speaking, no altered tones. In this respect the necessity of using accidentals to indicate certain pitches is misleading as they lack the conventional connotation of being raised or lowered from the basic scale. In this example the incidence of the various tones is particularly even. F-sharp and D-sharp occur most frequently—six times each, and F-natural and B-natural least—twice each. Exploiting the availability of the full duodecuple scale, Hindemith executes unusually effective approaches to the climax and the cadence.

Ex. 61   Symphony in E-flat p10   *Hindemith*

Melodies of this sort admittedly are more difficult to sing and remember than those in a strong conventional tonality, but once heard and learned they are equally powerful and logical. Moreover, in this style the risk of being trite and resorting to clichés is greatly reduced. This tune achieves to a high degree a sense of inevitability. Each note creates the impression of being in its proper place and indispensable; characteristics infinitely desirable in melodies of all periods and styles.

Example 62 is another illustrating the concept of free tonality. Though very different in contour from Example 61, their tonal aspects are remarkably similar with all twelve tones having equal freedom and importance in both.

Ex. 62   Symphony in E-flat p33   *Hindemith*

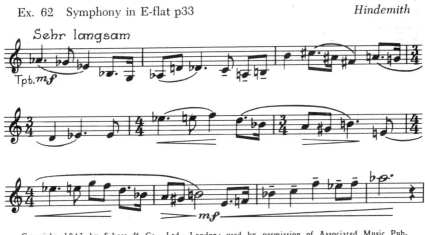

In the duodecuple scale equally tempered tuning is taken for granted, and the enharmonic spellings of notes are interchangeable. Accepted practice is to use the spelling which facilitates reading and playing, a practice Hindemith follows consistently.

Atonality, the tone row, and free tonality are all methods of exploiting more fully the latent possibilities of the duodecuple scale. All three have their place in the technical repertoire of the contemporary composer. There have been scattered experiments with tonal units smaller than the semitone as an additional source of melodic variety. As yet these experiments have exerted no real influence on the general course of Western music and do not rightly belong in a consideration of typical melodic practices up to the mid-century.

Contemporary Harmonic Influence

Just as the melodies of the classic and romantic periods frequently spell out their harmonies—triads and seventh chords—melodies of the present period use broken forms of more recent harmonic structures. The influence is less obvious because of the complexity of the harmonies, and the trend has been away from harmony as a stimulus for melodic invention. A few examples will suffice to illustrate the influence of contemporary harmony on melody.

Example 63 uses the broken form of a ninth chord on B-flat as a melodic line.

Ex. 63   String Quartet No. 5 p40   *Bartok*

Example 64 begins with an arpeggiation of a thirteenth chord on F. In this form the harmonic influence is apparent. The thirteenth chord, however, encompasses all the notes of C major. If the notes were arranged along scale line instead of along chord line, the harmonic implication would be missing. This possibility is most apparent in thirteenth chords, but it exists in all the more complex sonorities.

Ex. 64   Peter Grimes p27   *Britten*

The interval of the fourth was dormant as a harmonic ingredient, except in combination with certain other intervals, from the time of organum to the present century. The systematic use of chords built in fourths is an innovation of our time. Example 65 is evidence of fourth chord influence on melodic writing, the bulk of the melodic motion being perfect fourths.

Ex. 65   Concerto for Orchestra p1   *Bartok*

Example 66 is another using fourths, augmented and diminished as well as perfect, in the melodic line.

Ex. 66   Violin Concerto p7   *Barber*

When a contemporary harmonic idiom is adopted, its influence is almost certain to be manifest in the melodic writing. This is both natural and desirable. As with most practices it can be used to excess. Nothing is less interesting than a line derived exclusively from broken forms of the prevailing sonorities. Used judiciously in conjunction with scale-line and nonharmonic material, harmonic intervals add interest and variety to melodic lines.

Melodic Doubling

The doubling of melodic lines at intervals of the octave, third, and sixth has long been and continues to be common practice. Contemporary composers have added to these other intervals and complete chords. Doublings at conventional diatonic intervals are encountered too frequently in the pages of music both old and new to require comment. It is not to be inferred that their usefulness has been exhausted but rather that skill in their use has been acquired through previous study and familiarity with the standard music literature. Anyone deficient in this respect can find countless examples in the works of Brahms, for whom melodic doubling is almost a trademark, and in the works of most composers from the baroque period on. Only doublings which color and reinforce melodic lines in less conventional ways are illustrated.

The *Giuoco Delle Coppie* (second movement) of Bartok's *Concerto for Orchestra* is virtually a catalog of contemporary melodic doublings. It starts, after a brief introduction on the side drum, with two bassoons playing the melody in sixths.

Ex. 67   Concerto for Orchestra p29   *Bartok*

The consistent doubling at the minor sixth is broken only once in this excerpt. The doubling and the resulting false relations are characteristic features of the passage. Their significance becomes more apparent if the lines are played separately. The effect of doubling is more pronounced when the intervals are uniform than when they are diatonic with varied quality.

Immediately after the bassoon passage in sixths comes a section for oboes in thirds with the minor quality predominating.

Ex. 68   Concerto for Orchestra p30   *Bartok*

Unlike Examples 67 and 68 which are unconventional only in their emphasis on equal rather than diatonic intervals, Example 69 from the same work features doubling at a dissonant interval, the minor seventh.

Ex. 69   Concerto for Orchestra p30   *Bartok*

Doubling at the perfect fifth, strictly forbidden by conventional rules, is used in Example 70.

Ex. 70   Concerto for Orchestra p32   *Bartok*

This series of passages using in succession doublings at various intervals is brought to a close with two trumpets playing in parallel major seconds. One not already familiar with the passage might expect a dissonant effect, but this is not the case. The muted trumpets playing softly, as they do in Example 71, produce an interesting color which is not at all dissonant in the traditional sense.

Ex. 71   Concerto for Orchestra p34   *Bartok*

A performance or a good recording of Bartok's *Concerto for Orchestra* will bring these examples to life and vividly demonstrate some of the possibilities in contemporary melodic doubling. It is highly recommended listening for anyone not already familiar with this modern masterpiece.

Melodic doubling is not limited to single intervals. In his *First Symphony*, Milhaud doubles this Aeolian theme in diatonic triads.

Ex. 72   Symphony No. 1 p72   *Milhaud*

Used with the permission of the publishers Heugel & Cie., copyright owners, Paris.

A still more elaborate melodic doubling occurs in *The Rite of Spring*. The melody in Example 73 moves in diatonic seventh chords which have the third doubled and the fifth omitted.

Ex. 73   The Rite of Spring p39   *Stravinsky*

An extended melodic line doubled with ninth chords surely would prove to be monotonous, but sonorities with ninth chord implication have been used to double melodic fragments like that in Example 74 with good effect. The perception of these chords is somewhat obscured by their spacing, but they can be analyzed (ignoring the sustained A's) as ninth chords with the third omitted, reading from the top down-- fifth, ninth, root, and then seventh in each hand.

Ex. 74   Preludes Book II No. 2   *Debussy*

The technique of melodic doubling is one which should be used sparingly. The examples selected to demonstrate it are from isolated passages in larger works where the device was appropriate and effective. Its value is as a source of color and distinction, not as a substitute for quality in the basic melodic line.

Suggested Assignments

1. Illustrate each distinctive twentieth century melodic practice cited in the text with a melody copied from a contemporary composition. Other themes from the sources of the examples in the chapter may be used.
2. Write idiomatic melodies for various instruments exploiting some of the possibilities suggested in the section on nonvocal melodic lines.
3. Write melodies using scale patterns from the examples. Invent additional scales and compose melodies using them.
4. Write melodies exploiting the principles of free tonality. In these pay particular attention to contour, organization, and to the element of unity which is apt to be lacking.
5. Write melodic lines influenced by contemporary harmonic structures.
6. Listen to a recording of the second movement of Bartok's *Concerto for Orchestra*. Analyze the intervals between parts involved in melodic doublings by ear or from the score.
7. Devise effective doublings for original or borrowed melodies. Original melodies may be drawn from previous assignments.

CHAPTER V

Harmonic Structure

Harmonic structure is the vertical arrangement of notes sounding simultaneously. These harmonic sounds occur rarely as an isolated phenomenon, but a thorough understanding of chord structure is necessary before considering the more complex problem of harmonic progression.

Knowledge of conventional harmonic structures is presupposed. These include all of the diatonic triads and seventh chords with their inversions and alterations. Since these are basic materials of the conventional harmonic vocabulary, they are excluded from this study. It is not that triads and seventh chords are obsolete. On the contrary, many passages in recent works do not go beyond these harmonic means. However, a more complex harmonic language is required to express contemporary musical ideas. This has caused the tremendous expansion in the harmonic vocabulary and not the search for novelty which is sometimes suspected.

When first hearing music in the more advanced twentieth century idioms, one sometimes gets the impression modern composers have severed all ties with tradition and the traditional music which makes up the greater part of concert programs, broadcasts, and recordings. This break is more apparent than real. The development of harmonic resources has followed a course of exploiting ever higher and higher reaches of the overtone series. In this, contemporary composers are merely continuing a process which started with magadizing and organum and led successively to triads, seventh, ninth, eleventh, thirteenth chords, and beyond. The enrichment of harmonic resources through the successive inclusion of higher members of the overtone series is şhown in the following example.

Ex. 75   The overtone series

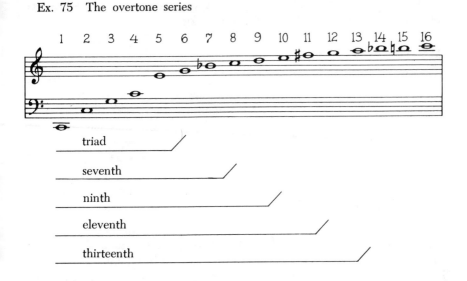

All dissonant sonorities, even the minor ninth chord, involve the use of pitches above the sixteenth partial. They are produced by exploiting relationships which exist between the higher members of the overtone series. Though the process by which harmonic resources are extended is established by tradition, the speed with which new sounds have been added in the recent past is remarkable. The most active chord fully accepted before the turn of the century was the dominant seventh, which occurs in the first seven tones of the overtone series. More complex chords were used sporadically before this, but now sonorities embracing the relationships of the higher members of the series are an integral part of every composer's harmonic language.

The pitches of many overtones are only approximated in equally tempered tuning. Even seven and eleven of the series are not represented accurately. Because of its practical advantages equal temperament has achieved universal recognition, at least as far as keyboard instruments and notation are concerned. For this reason enharmonic spellings are frequently used to facilitate reading, and they are used in this chapter to simplify analysis.

In the following examples representative chord structures selected from twentieth century works are given, usually in brief context. When necessary to make the underlying structure more apparent, the chord components are rearranged and shown in root position with close spacing and enharmonic spelling in whole notes. Corresponding numbers identify the chords under consideration and their simplified versions. This type of analysis and descriptions of chord formations are used in the absence of any convenient, standard terminology for contemporary sonorities.

Superimposed Thirds

Contemporary chords built in thirds are most closely related to conventional harmonies since they continue the process by which triads and seventh chords are constructed, superimposition of thirds. The study of conventional harmony usually encompasses all diatonic triad and seventh chord structures in major and minor keys though some of them, such as minor and augmented triads with major sevenths, are rare in traditional music. Chromatic alteration was used prior to the present century to make various chord structures available on each degree of the scale but not to create new harmonic formations.

Chromatic alteration of the notes in conventional seventh chords can produce new structures like that of the first chord in Example 76. Observe how effectively this chord progresses to the dominant seventh*. The B-flat in the last chord of the example appears in the score as a B-flat and also enharmonically as an A-sharp. Either way it is an unconventional spelling of a familiar sound.

Ex. 76   Piano Concerto No. 3 p10   *Bartok*

There are several other possibilities for seventh chord structures which do not occur diatonically. One favored by Gershwin consists of a diminished triad with a major seventh. Unfortunately, examples from Gershwin cannot be given because of copyright restrictions.

The addition of a third above the seventh produces a ninth chord. This structure was first used on the fifth degree of the scale, that is, as a dominant ninth. It soon became common on other scale degrees. Diatonically, the ninth of the dominant is major in major keys and minor

---

*Dominant seventh is used in this chapter to denote the chord structure of a major triad with a minor seventh, and not dominant function in a key.

in minor keys. Both of these forms are still very much a part of the harmonic language of popular music, so much so that serious composers tend to view them askance nowadays. They have, nevertheless, figured prominently in music of the twentieth century, especially during the early part and in the music of the impressionist composers. Example 77 shows the dominant major ninth structure in its most usual arrangement with the root in the bass and the ninth in the soprano.

Ex. 77   Pelleas and Melisande p7   *Debussy*

Another example of the dominant major ninth in the same position demonstrates that its use is not limited to the impressionists and the first part of the century.

Ex. 78   Te Deum p8   *Kodaly*

Other inversions and positions of ninth chords such as those shown in Example 79 are not uncommon. Each chord contains the interval of a ninth, but probably only that in the first and third measures would be perceived as a ninth chord.

Ex. 79   Pelleas and Melisande p78   *Debussy*

The dominant minor ninth is illustrated in Example 80. In the last chord Bloch spells the third enharmonically as G-flat. The fifths frequently are omitted from ninth chords as they are here.

Ex. 80   Violin Sonata p60   *Bloch*

Ninths are used with chord structures other than the dominant seventh. Example 81 has two ninth chords, the first built on a minor triad.

Ex. 81   Bagatelle No. 1   *Tcherepnine*

The harmonic implication of the first measure in Example 82 seems to be a ninth chord on F-sharp. Though the notes do not occur simultaneously, all appear and only the D-sharp is foreign to this harmony. A dominant ninth on E and its resolution occupy the second measure, with the C-sharp sounding like an unresolved nonchord tone. The vertical arrangement on the first beat with the ninth below the third and seventh is unusual.

Ex. 82   Piano Sonatine p3   *Ravel*

Ninth chords frequently appear in passages where tonality is vague. In such passages they gain in interest and in freedom of progression. Ninth chords contribute to the dissipation of tonality when they do not resolve in a conventional manner. This is especially true when they progress by parallel motion to another ninth chord. Example 83 illustrates this usage.

Ex. 83   Preludes Book II No. 2   *Debussy*

The ninth chord on C-sharp in Example 84 has the structure but not the function of a dominant. The G-sharp minor chord following has a ninth, A-sharp, but is not a ninth chord strictly speaking, because it lacks a seventh.

Ex. 84   The Lament for Beowulf p36   *Hanson*

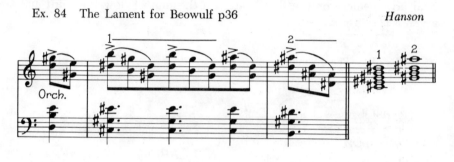

Ninths used with major, minor, and augmented triads have been illustrated. A further possibility is demonstrated in Example 85 which is like a dominant major ninth with a flat fifth. The flat fifth, D-flat, also is spelled enharmonically as C-sharp.

Ex. 85   Preludes Book II No. 10   *Debussy*

Ninth chords, especially those other than the dominant ninth, can be spaced in ways which obscure their underlying structure. This is true in Example 86. The ear can scarcely detect the tertial derivation of these sonorities. The perception of chord 2 as a ninth chord is complicated by the major seventh and the omission of the third.

Ex. 86   Piano Concerto p95   *Ravel*

These examples show only representative ninth chords, and there
are many other possibilities. Major and minor ninths may be added to
all the seventh chord structures, both diatonic and altered. The dominant ninth was the first to be incorporated into the harmonic vocabulary,
but its value now to serious composers is impaired by popular connotations and triteness. Other less hackneyed ninth chord forms are currently in favor. Their pungent sounds are still capable of expressiveness
when used with imagination, even to the jaded ears of the twentieth
century.

The addition of another third above a ninth produces an eleventh
chord. Like the ninth, these appeared first on the fifth degree of the
scale as dominants, but subsequently were employed on other scale
degrees and in other forms. Example 87 is a strong, tonal cadence in
C major with a supertonic eleventh and a dominant eleventh going to a
tonic with an added sixth. The spacing of the score is preserved.

Ex. 87   Petrouchka p61   *Stravinsky*

The elevenths in the previous example are diatonic, but the sharp
or augmented eleventh is used more frequently. Actually, the eleventh

note of the overtone series comes between these two notes of the equally tempered system. The augmented eleventh seems to produce the richer sound. It is a great favorite with jazz composers and arrangers and is not without its merits in serious music. Example 88 has the augmented eleventh with a minor ninth, written enharmonically as C-sharp in the violin part for easier reading. The omission of the chord fifth in this example and in similar structures does not alter the total effect appreciably.

Ex. 88   Violin Sonata p23   *Bloch*

The examples illustrate typical eleventh chords, but elevenths may be added to all of the ninth chord structures. Experimentation will reveal which alterations, spacing, and inversions are most effective.

Continuing the process of building chords in superimposed thirds leads, with the addition of a third to the eleventh chord, to the thirteenth chord. A diatonic thirteenth chord contains every note of the scale, but more often than not there is some chromatic alteration. A thirteenth chord with an augmented eleventh, illustrated in Example 89, is one of the most common forms.

Ex. 89   Piano Concerto p73   *Ravel*

Bloch utilizes an identical structure in his violin sonata. Three versions of the same basic chord are illustrated in Examples 90, 91, and 92. Examples 90 and 91 are from adjoining passages. Example 92 is from the following movement.

Ex. 90   Violin Sonata p42   *Bloch*

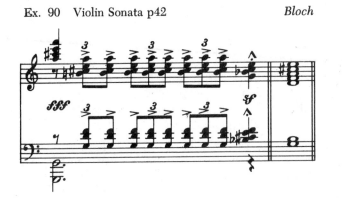

Ex. 91   Violin Sonata p43   *Bloch*

Ex. 92   Violin Sonata p49   *Bloch*

As with the other tertial sonorities, thirteenths may be added to all of the previous structures. Inclusion of seven tones in a single chord allows almost infinite variation in spacing and inversion producing many degrees of resonance and dissonance. Since a thirteenth chord consists of a complete circle of thirds, any tonal member may be considered the root from a standpoint of abstract structure. For this reason the true root can be determined only on the basis of the sound. Consequently the bass most often is perceived as the root when thirds predominate in the spacing. When the chord members are arranged to emphasize seconds and fourths, which is equally possible, the same notes may be quite lacking in tertial implication.

The tone a third above the thirteenth is a duplication of the root two octaves higher. To construct chords in thirds beyond the thirteenth, one must resort to double inflections. That is, a natural note and the same note with a flat or sharp must be used. Double inflections are not uncommon, but tertial sonorities with all seven tones plus double inflections are extremely rare and of limited usefulness. They are found in isolated passages of a few works such as Gershwin's *Porgy and Bess*.

Students accustomed to writing within the bounds of academic harmony discover a new and exciting realm in ninth, eleventh, and thirteenth chords. This threshold is not crossed without forfeiting some advantages of simple chord structures. The essential characteristics of conventional chords remain intact through a wide range of inversions, spacings, and doublings. This is less true of even slightly more dissonant harmonies. For example, relatively few inversions and spacings of major seventh and minor ninth chords are suitable for normal expressive purposes though the range of different sounds obtainable is vastly augmented by the addition of these dissonant elements. As harmonic complexity increases the arrangement of chord components becomes more and more circumscribed.

Formulation of precise rules applicable to all complex sonorities is not possible, but the overtone series provides a convenient and generally valid guide. Complicated chords are most resonant in root position with wider intervals below and narrower intervals above, as they occur in the overtone series. Within this spacing greater resonance results when the lower partials of the chord root are toward the bass and the higher partials are toward the soprano, approximating their location in the series. Other arrangements tend to inhibit the resonance and sharpen the dissonance of any tonal combination. Distributing chord members according to the overtone series is merely a rule of thumb, not an inviolable principle. Unusual inversions and spacings are required on occasion to produce a desired effect. In the final analysis a composer must rely upon his ear, imagination, and taste in these matters as in everything else.

Chords of more than four tones, not counting octave doublings, are inclined to be thick and cumbersome, and nothing palls faster than a composition overladen with ninth, eleventh, and thirteenth chords. A more serious problem is that such chords virtually eliminate the possibility of vigorous counterpoint. Every note of a seven-tone scale is contained in a thirteenth chord, so melodic lines within the key can only go from one chord tone to another. Notes outside the key, being no more than a half step from one of the chord tones, merely sound like neighboring tones. Because of these limitations and because such lush sounds are out of vogue, chords beyond the seventh built in thirds are comparatively rare in recent music. Related sonorities which preserve their advantages and avoid their shortcomings are better suited to contemporary requirements.

Chords of Addition and Omission

These apparently contradictory terms are applied to a group of closely related sonorities. Many of the chords falling in these classifications may be analyzed in either way, depending upon the point of view, as will be shown in the analysis.

A simple chord to which is added one or more notes normally foreign but used as an integral part of the sonority is designated a *chord of addition*. A more complex chord from which one or more normally essential elements is omitted is designated a *chord of omission*. Added and omitted notes are identified by the interval above the root of the basic chord.

The most obvious example of a chord of addition is the *tonic added sixth*.

Ex. 93   The Song of the Earth p159   *Mahler*

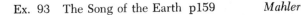

The same structure also occurs as a supertonic seventh in the first inversion, but coming as the final chord of a work, as it does in this example, its function is clear. The tonic added sixth as a cadence chord has long since lost its freshness through prodigal use by popular composers and arrangers. It is still a valid manifestation of a process through which many current sonorities are derived. Since this structure has the added sixth implication only when it is used as a cadence chord, it occurs only on the tonic.

Another added note which is used in popular music but which is regarded somewhat more highly by serious composers is the added second.

Ex. 94   Te Deum p15   *Kodaly*

This structure could be analyzed as a ninth chord with the seventh omitted, but the effect of the ninth is altered greatly by the omission of the seventh. In the absence of the seventh its consideration as a chord of addition seems preferable. On the other hand, if the fifth were omitted instead of the seventh, the effect would be very close to that of a complete ninth chord.

The sixth and second are both added to a major triad in Example 95.

Ex. 95   American Ballads No. 1 p5   *Harris*

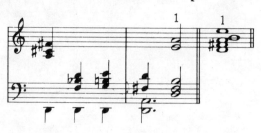

The second is also added to minor triads with good effect.

Ex. 96   Pelleas and Melisande p6   *Debussy*

Example 97 shows a major triad with an added second progressing to a dominant thirteenth with the eleventh omitted or a dominant ninth with a sixth added.

Ex. 97   Preludes Book II No. 10   *Debussy*

The omission of the third evokes the greatest change in the effect of a chord. If the bass is analyzed as the roots, the chords in Example 98 are ninth chords with the thirds omitted. They may also be analyzed as major triads with added perfect fourths. In this analysis the added notes are below the triads unlike any of the previous examples. Since added notes are most often above the basic chord, the former analysis seems preferable.

Ex. 98   Violin Sonata p13   *Copland*

Added notes are not always in a diatonic relationship to the underlying chord. Any note may be added. Example 99 illustrates the use
of an added augmented fourth above a major triad, both spelled enharmonically in the analysis for greater clarity.

Ex. 99   Te Deum p13   *Kodaly*

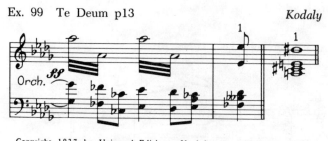

A more sophisticated added-note chord is used by Bloch in his
Violin Sonata. At the close of the second movement, after firmly estab-
lishing the tonality of B-flat minor, he uses a B-flat minor triad with an
added sixth for the cadence chord, to which later are added the major
seventh and the augmented fourth.

Ex. 100   Violin Sonata p47   *Bloch*

Sometimes the added note is another inflection of a note present in the basic chord as in Example 101 with both a major and a minor third.

Ex. 101   Peter Grimes p2   *Britten*

When both the major and the minor third are present in a chord, the minor third usually is placed above the major third as it is here.

Three chords of addition or omission over the same root are used in Example 102: a minor triad with an added second, a dominant seventh structure with both major and minor thirds, and a thirteenth chord with the third and eleventh omitted.

Ex. 102   American Ballads No. 4   *Harris*

These examples show some typical chords of addition and omission. Many more are possible, and this process places at the disposal of the composer an infinite variety of sonorities with an unusually wide range of consonance and dissonance. Sonorities of this type have the added advantage of a close link with tradition in their underlying basic chord. Sounds with a perceptible relation to conventional chords have more appeal for average listeners than obtuse tonal combinations, an advantage not to be overlooked by a composer still seeking recognition and without assured performances.

When three notes or more are added to a chord, they more often than not assume the form of another chord. This leads to the next classification of harmonic sounds, those that result from combining simple chords.

Polychords

Sonorities which can best be understood as combinations of conventional chords are designated *polychords*. Only triads and seventh chords are united in polychordal formations. Less familiar structures loose their identity in complex associations. The elements of individual chords within a polychord are united with each other and isolated from those of other chords by means of color, range, and/or spacing to emphasize the distinctive polychord quality.

In a sense every seventh chord is a combination of two triads. The dominant seventh in the key of C can be analyzed as a major triad on G combined with a diminished triad on B. All seventh chords can be considered combinations of various types of triads with roots a third apart. Applying this manner of analysis to ninth chords, it is apparent that each ninth chord encompasses three triads and two seventh chords. Eleventh chords encompass four triads, three seventh chords, and two ninth chords, and thirteenth chords encompass five triads, four seventh chords, three ninth chords, and two eleventh chords. As long as there are common tones and a close relationship between the triads, they are perceived as components of a single chord unless widely separated in register or scored in contrasting colors. The polychordal implications of such chords can be stressed deliberately by separation in register and by contrast in color.

Though interesting effects are possible exploiting the polychordal implications of ninth, eleventh, and thirteenth chords, remote polychordal associations are most attractive. One of the first to be used joined major triads a tritone apart. This polychord figures prominently in *Petrouchka*, and the augmented fourth-diminished fifth relationship has thematic significance in the work. While trumpets and cornets play the C major figure in Example 103, horns sustain the F-sharp major triad and strings, woodwinds, and piano rapidly alternate the two triads.

Ex. 103   Petrouchka p65   *Stravinsky*

The sonority resulting from two major triads at the distance of a tritone is not so remote from those considered previously as might be expected. The sounds of Example 103 can be rearranged and spelled enharmonically as a dominant minor ninth with an augmented eleventh.

Ex. 104

The visual impression of complex chords can be changed by enharmonic spellings. The spelling of a particular chord is influenced by the way it is used, and the analysis is influenced in turn by the spelling. Such distinctions are of no great importance when dealing with isolated harmonic structures, but the spelling used by the composer is taken into account in the following analyses. The reductions are designed to reveal the underlying structure. Other interpretations are possible in some cases.

Hanson uses the augmented fourth relationship between two dominant seventh type chords in his *Romantic Symphony*. The chord is scored for full orchestra with the spacing as shown first.

Ex. 105   Symphony No. 2 (Romantic) p39   *Hanson*

The augmented fourth relationship is only one of the possibilities. Harris makes an effective final cadence with major triads at the interval of a major third.

Ex. 106   American Ballads No. 4   *Harris*

Ravel uses a G major triad and a D-sharp minor seventh together in a piano figuration.

Ex. 107   Piano Concerto p1   *Ravel*

Later in the same work a minor and a major triad with roots a major seventh apart are combined in a polychord.

Ex. 108   Piano Concerto p91   *Ravel*

In Example 109 varied relationships—major seventh, perfect fifth, major third, and major second—result from two streams of major triads in contrary motion.

Ex. 109   Three Score Set No. II   *Schuman*

The major triads in the previous example at the intervals of a major seventh and a perfect fifth produce chords which can also be analyzed as eleventh and ninth chords respectively. However, the polychords analysis is supported in this instance by the harmonic streams.

One of the most complex polychords occurs in *The Rite of Spring* where a major triad and a dominant seventh structure with roots a major seventh apart are combined. The scoring is homogeneous. The complete polychord in the spacing shown is played by divisi strings reinforced on the accents by eight horns. After eight measures of the block chord, broken forms of these same two chords (F-flat major now spelled enharmonically as E major) are combined with a third chord— a C major triad.

Ex. 110   The Rite of Spring p11   *Stravinsky*

The process of combining conventional chord structures in poly-chords adds rich harmonic colors to the composer's pallette. This means of developing sonorities is capable of producing infinite shades of dis-'sonance. As with most complex sonorities the effect depends as much upon position, spacing, register, and scoring as upon pitch components. In these matters the overtone series is less efficient as a guide for poly-chords, since they draw material from two sources, than for tertial chord structures. Testing various polychord combinations at the piano provides experience in selecting effective relationships, spacings, and registers. Studying scores and listening to records of works containing polychords serves to illustrate the effects of orchestral coloring in the absence of opportunities to hear one's own instrumental compositions.

Nontertial Sonorities

Chords built in superimposed thirds along with various additions to and combinations of such chords have been studied. Another fertile source of twentieth century harmonic material lies in the direction of sonorities constructed in intervals other than thirds. These are consid-ered collectively as *nontertial* sonorities.

Nontertial sonorities are not without ancestors in more conventional chords. The second inversion of a triad with a seven-six suspension in the soprano gives a chord in fourths. When the seventh, root, and ninth of a ninth chord appear in close position in that order, a segment of a chord in seconds results. The thirteenth chord, since it contains all of the tones of a seven note scale, can be arranged in seconds, fourths, and fifths as well as in thirds. Regarded in this way nontertial sonorities rep-resent a logical manner of extending harmonic resources along lines suggested in more conventional harmonies and sometimes existing in embryonic form in traditional practices.

The augmented triad which results from combining alternate notes of the whole tone scale also exists in conventional harmony as the mediant triad in harmonic minor. Within the limitations of the whole tone scale, only three-note chords can be constructed in thirds except through the use of a diminished third which sounds like a major second. Some of the earliest implications of nontertial sonorities resulted when four-note chords were constructed from the whole tone scale.

Ex. 111   Pelleas and Melisande p3   *Debussy*

As the chords are spelled in Example 111, the nontertial implication is apparent only in the first, but that both have the same underlying structure can be demonstrated by enharmonic spelling. The first would have the same pattern as the second if spelled F, A, C-sharp, E-flat, and conversely, the second would have the same pattern as the first if spelled A, B, C-sharp, E-sharp. This chord structure is commonly designated the *whole tone dominant*.

After one conventional dominant seventh chord, Example 112 consists of a series of these whole tone dominants. While the last one is sustained, an F-sharp is added in the bass and a D appears in the repeated note figure, so all six notes of the whole tone scale are sounding simultaneously.

Ex. 112   Preludes Book I No. 6   *Debussy*

The use of chords in seconds is not restricted to the impressionists nor the whole tone scale. Seconds are prominent in the harmonies of Example 113, though the sustained notes in the violin perhaps should be considered pedal notes rather than chord tones.

Ex. 113   Violin Sonata p13   *Copland*

Seconds are used in a quite different fashion in Example 114.

Ex. 114   Mikrokosmos Vol. IV No. 107   *Bartok*

When three or more consecutive scale steps occur simultaneously, the resulting structure is known as a *cluster*. Extended clusters are better suited to the piano than to other instruments though they are possible and do occur occasionally in other media. Example 115 shows seven-note clusters on the white keys alternating rapidly with the five notes of the black keys, together comprising all the notes of a chromatic octave.

Ex. 115   Piano Concerto No. 2 p57   *Bartok*

A cluster on the black keys is followed by a cluster on the white keys in the excerpt from the accompaniment of a Charles Ives song.

Ex. 116   Song: Majority   *Ives*

Strangely enough such conglomerations of notes as these are not dissonant in the conventional sense. They neither sound active nor demand resolution. Used sparingly and with discretion clusters add a curious bit of color to the harmonic repertoire. They had the added advantage of being novel a few decades ago, but their effect rapidly becomes vapid. No longer capable of creating a sensation, they are rarely found in more recent works.

Contemporary composers also make use of sonorities in which fourths are the primary interval.   These chords generally lack the resonance of the tertial sonorities because their components, being in a less direct relationship with the overtones of the root, are reinforced less by them. This is particularly true when all of the fourths are perfect and when fourths are only the intervals in the structure. Consequently, fourth chords ordinarily are not used exclusively throughout a composition or even for an extended passage. Used in conjunction with other types of harmony and for brief passages, they provide an extremely useful harmonic color.

La Cathédrale Engloutie is a familiar work which makes extensive use of chords in fourths. Both the sustained chord in Example 117 and those moving in quarter notes are constructed essentially in fourths, with only the third of the quarter-note chords excepted. Observe that seconds result from octave doublings in fourth chords.

Ex. 117   Preludes Book 1 No. 10   *Debussy*

Permission for reprint granted by Durand & Cie., Paris, France, copyright owners; Elkan-Vogel Co., Inc., Philadelphia, Pa., agents.

When one of the fourths is inverted and becomes a fifth, as in the whole note chord of the previous example, the lower member asserts itself as the root and tends to create the impression of a tertial sonority with the third omitted. For this reason the interval of the fifth directly above the bass is avoided when the distinctive fourth-chord quality is desired.

Berg runs the gamut of chord construction in perfect fourths, from two notes to seven, in *Wozzeck*. Since all of the voices move parallel, this perhaps should be considered merely melodic doubling. It cannot be regarded as a typical example of chord progression, but it illustrates with unusual clarity extended structures in perfect fourths, though some are notated as augmented thirds.

Ex. 118   Wozzeck p70   *Berg*

A more varied use of fourth chords is shown in Example 119. The basic chords are built in perfect fourths, with contrary motion and moving parts adding interest.

Ex. 119   Song: Majority   *Ives*

Though it hardly would be suspected from the sound, the final chord in Schoenberg's piano piece is written in fourths, one of them perfect and the other two augmented. Chords containing augmented or diminished fourths bear little resemblance in sound to those constructed in perfect fourths.

Ex. 120   Three Piano Pieces Op. 11 No 1.   *Schoenberg*

Scriabin's mystic chord has an unusually interesting structure using perfect, augmented, and diminished fourths.

Ex. 121   Mystic Chord   *Scriabin*

Chords built entirely in fifths are rare, but they do occur. One such instance is in *The Rite of Spring* where the following six-note chord in perfect fifths is used.

Ex. 122   The Rite of Spring p13   *Stravinsky*

The first chord of Example 123 has the same structure as the previous example after which the harmony breaks into two streams of three-note chords in fifths moving in contrary motion.

Ex. 123   Piano Concerto No. 2 p44   *Bartok*

The final chord of Example 124 is another six-note chord in fifths, one of them diminished. The notes of the left hand must be placed above those of the right to preserve the spacing in fifths throughout.

Ex. 124   Three Piano Pieces Op. 11 No. 2   *Schoenberg*

Chord structures stressing perfect fourths and fifths are used in *The Lament for Beowulf* to evoke the archaic atmosphere of the text. Only an outline of the harmonic background is given. These chords are repeated in a rhythmic pattern in the original as a background for the vocal lines.

Ex. 125   The Lament for Beowulf p6   *Hanson*

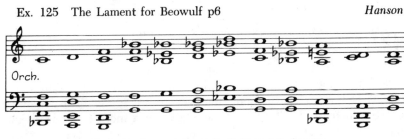

A chord in fourths progresses to a chord in fifths in Example 126. Only part of the melody notes are included in the fourth and fifth structures.

Ex. 126   Three Piano Pieces Op. 11 No. 2   *Schoenberg*

Example 127, which shows the harmonic outline of a section of a Bartok quartet, employs some conventional structures and some discussed in this chapter between a chord in fifths and a chord in fourths. The chords are spaced first as in the original and then in a manner which makes their underlying structure more apparent.

Ex. 127   String Quartet No. 5 p50   *Bartok*

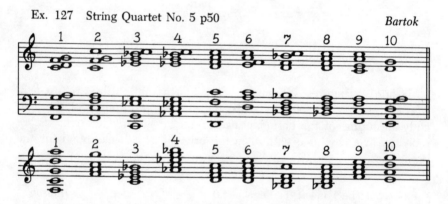

It is when manifold possibilities for harmonic structure are exploited simultaneously, as they are in Example 127, rather than when types are isolated that maximum effectiveness is achieved. This has been suggested in these brief examples, and it is even more apparent in the complete works.

Suggested Assignments

1. Reduce the harmonic structures of Debussy's *Prelude Book I No. 10* to their simplest form, and classify them according to the categories used in this chapter.

2. Analyze selected excerpts from Stravinsky's *Petrouchka* in the manner of Assignment 1. Examples 87 and 103 may serve as points of departure.

3. Locate characteristic harmonic structures in other contemporary compositions. Observe their spacing and doubling, and then rearrange them to reveal their underlying harmonic structures.

4. Write sonorities in each category discussed in this chapter—superimposed thirds, addition and omission, polychords, and nontertial. First give the basic structure and then several effective arrangements paying careful attention to spacing, doubling, and choice of bass. Strive for variety of effect in the different versions of each basic chord.

CHAPTER **VI**

Harmonic Progression

The harmonic structures explored in Chapter V are like individual words. As words realize their full significance when used with other words in sentences, chords realize their full significance when used with other chords in *progressions*.

Harmonic progression, like harmonic structure, is characterized by great freedom in the twentieth century. Most of the restrictions recognized in the conventional, tonal writing of the eighteenth and nineteenth centuries and scrupulously observed by the composers of those periods are now regarded as arbitrary. Discarding artificial prohibitions enriches the permissible harmonic structures and progressions enormously. It is not an exaggeration to state that in our time every harmonic relationship as well as every harmonic structure is allowed. This could lead to chaos, but more often freedom of harmonic progression is exercised along logical lines which yield to analysis.

To understand and appreciate the current freedom in harmonic progression, the restrictions previously imposed must be recognized. Major-minor tonality and progresssion according to fundamental bass dominated the musical thinking of almost three centuries. Major-minor tonality implies a rather rigid adherence to two seven-note scale patterns with certain triad and seventh-chord structures associated with each position in the scale. The limited variety inherent in the three forms of the minor scale is reduced by the preference for the harmonic and melodic forms which borrow essential features from major. These scale patterns provided the basic chord structures and relationships, and all others occurred incidentally in secondary roles.

A strong sense of tonality was a universally recognized and practiced concept in Western music. This feeling for the tonal center was fostered by an emphasis upon movements of chord roots in fourths and fifths, the relationships most conducive to tonality. Modulations were usually made to related keys according to prescribed formulas.

These limitations are not always apparent. One is never bothered by the fact that Mozart is working within the confines of the major-minor system. It is a tribute to his genius that he created such epic works with restricted resources and perhaps a recognition of our own limitations that obliges us to add perpetually to the materials.

Harmonic resources were never completely static. Even during the extended period dominated by major-minor tonality and restricted fundamental bass movement, new harmonic concepts were evolving continually if slowly. The process was hastened by Wagner, and just before the turn of the century, it erupted dramatically.

To facilitate comprehension of contemporary harmonic progressions, they are considered here in various categories and in connection with the simpler harmonic structures. In actual usage no such isolation exists, and all of the progressions and relationships are possible with sophisticated as well as with simple structures.

Modal Quality

In the matter of harmonic progression, as in melodic materials, contemporary composers have not neglected a re-examination of the modes in their unending quest for additional resources. Since the earlier exploitations of modal materials were largely melodic and contrapuntal, their harmonic possibilities are far from exhausted, and they have provided a valuable means of extending the horizons of tonal organization in the twentieth century. Besides the passages couched more or less in pure modal terms, many others bear witness to modal influences.

From a standpoint of chord structure, the modes do not make available any sound not also possible in major or minor. It is in the relationship of these sounds and in their function that the modal influence is apparent. In the major-minor system the progression and resolution of altered notes and chromatic harmonies traditionally are subject to resolution in the direction of alteration, which results in stereotyped voice leading and harmonic progression. These traditions no doubt stem from conditioning more than from any natural inclination, but they constitute a force which must be reckoned with in writing for audiences thoroughly indoctrinated in conventional tonal practices. By making these same sounds available with diatonic notes, the modes provide an effective antidote for stereotypes and free harmonic progression from onerous encumbrances.

Each mode offers a different set of harmonic values within diatonic limits. This immediately increases many times the subtle harmonic relationships possible without resorting to chromatic alteration and submitting to its attendant restrictions. In addition, it tends to overthrow the tyranny of the dominant-tonic relationship of tonal music, especially in the modes having a minor dominant or with the dominant function on a scale degree other than the fifth.

Each diatonic mode contains three major triads, three minor triads, and one diminished triad, but the arrangement is different. The following table gives the dispositions of the various qualities of triads in each mode:

QUALITY OF THE TRIADS IN THE MODES

Mode	Tonic	Supertonic	Mediant	Subdominant	Dominant	Submediant	Subtonic
Ionian	major	minor	minor	major	major	minor	diminished
Dorian	minor	minor	major	major	minor	diminished	major
Phrygian	minor	major	major	minor	diminished	major	minor
Lydian	major	major	minor	diminished	major	minor	minor
Mixolydian	major	minor	diminished	major	minor	minor	major
Aeolian	minor	diminished	major	minor	minor	major	major
Locrian	diminished	major	minor	minor	major	major	minor

Just as each mode has a distinctive pattern of triad relationships, each has a unique arrangement of seventh chord qualities and all other harmonic structures. The following examples illustrate some of the ways modal resources have been tapped by contemporary composers. The primary concern at this point is to show the variety of relationship in chord quality through the use of the modes, but observe that this freedom also extends to the root relationships.

The melody of Example 128 could be either Aeolian or Dorian on D since the sixth degree of the scale is not used. The accompaniment, mostly in triads, is predominantly Dorian, using the B-flat which would make it Aeolian only in the fifth measure. The final chord is made major, a common practice in both modal and tonal music.

Ex. 128   Concerto Gregoriano p9   *Respighi*

The harmony becomes more complicated as the voices are added in Example 129, but all remain in Dorian on A for the duration of the excerpt. The tonic is vague at the end, but the whole passage comes over a pedal A in the orchestra (not shown) which fixes the tonal center and the mode.

Ex. 129   The Vision of Sir Launfal p36   *Sowerby*

Example 130 is Barlow's setting of a Dorian folk song on A. The accompaniment, too, is essentially Dorian with only one G-sharp and the F-naturals deviating from the pure mode. Seventh-chord structures predominate. This example, like number 128, closes with a major triad as many modal pieces of earlier periods did.

Ex. 130   The Winter's Past p6   *Barlow*

The Phrygian mode on G is illustrated in Example 131. The mode is pure except for the F-sharp in the penultimate chord, and even here the characteristic flat second degree of the scale is preserved.

Ex. 131   String Quartet p 1   *Debussy*

Because the Lydian mode is so similar in effect to major, it is difficult to isolate. The characteristic degree of Lydian, sharp four, occurs so frequently as a chromatic note in major differentiation between them is problematical. Example 132 is typical. The tonality is A, and both D-sharp and D-natural are used. Ignoring the signature, either could be regarded as the diatonic scale tone. The use of D-sharp in the repeated notes of measure 9 and in the descending figure of measures 12-14 imparts a Lydian flavor to the passage, and considering it as Lydian the D-naturals in each case can be heard as the altered tones.

Ex. 132   Symphony No. 4 p38   *Sibelius*

The Mixolydian mode, with its characteristic lowered seventh, is more readily distinguished and occurs in an obvious manner more frequently. Example 133 is a setting of a folk song with both the melody and the accompaniment in pure Mixolydian on E.

Ex. 133   The Winter's Past p2   *Barlow*

Example 134 is another in the pure Mixolydian mode, this one on G.
The two middle voices mirror the top voice.

Ex. 134   String Quartet No. 1 p23   *Thompson*

The Aeolian mode exists in conventional music as the natural minor, but when used in its pure form it has a decided modal flavor. The simple Aeolian harmonies are particularly effective in Example 135.

Ex. 135   The Medium p48   *Menotti*

Melodies in the Locrian mode are rare, and because of the diminished quality of its tonic triad harmonic examples in this mode are even rarer. Example 136, however, appears to be an instance of its use. The problem of the diminished tonic triad is avoided by dropping out all the voices but one and ending the phrase with the tonic note D alone.

Ex. 136   A Ceremony of Carols No. 8   *Britten*

Change of Mode—Free Relation of Quality

The new relationships available within individual modes are only the beginning. The number of possible relationships becomes almost infinite when major, minor, and all the modes are used interchangeably.

The interchangeability of minor and major is time-honored. Frequently used altered chords in major are borrowed from minor and vice versa. The major dominant is traditional in minor, and the major tonic at the close of compositions in minor was a convention of the sixteenth century which has never been abandoned. A contemporary usage of alternating minor and major tonic triads is shown in Example 137.

Ex. 137   A Ceremony of Carols No. 4b   *Britten*

If the principle of mode change is extended to embrace harmonies on all scale degrees and in all modes, each structure becomes available on every scale degree through substitution of mode without becoming subject to the restrictions implicit in chromatic alteration. A glance at the table of modal triads in this chapter shows that all three qualities—major, minor, and diminished—occur on every degree of the scale in one or more of the modes.

Example 138 has progressions which cannot be accounted for by conventional means of analysis but which are readily explained by changes of mode. In the analysis the pedal note A is somewhat arbitrarily designated the tonic, though the tonality is admittedly vague. Some of the structures are common to two, three, or four modes, but others are peculiar to one.

Ex. 138   Violin Concerto p5   *Khachaturian*

In his book *The Diatonic Modes in Modern Music**[*]* John Vincent has thoroughly explored change of mode with reference to triads and seventh chords. Obviously the principle can also be applied to ninth and eleventh chords and to all of the structures discussed in the previous chapter. However, composers writing music and listeners hearing it do not stop to classify each chord according to its derivation. In practice the result is a free association of chord qualities and structures without rationalizing their sources.

The following examples illustrate how contemporary composers have exploited free relation of quality between simple chord structures. The same procedures and relationships are equally feasible with complex chord formations.

The final cadence of *The Lament for Beowulf* makes effective use of free relation in quality between triads in root position. There are no taboos against false relations in contemporary practice. On the contrary,

---

[*]University of California Press, 1951.

there are many passages in which false relations are featured, as they are in Example 139.

Ex. 139   The Lament for Beowulf p44   *Hanson*

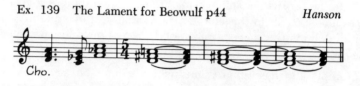

Cho.

Stravinsky interposes D-flat and E-flat major triads between F major triads in Example 140. Contrary motion in the outer parts adds to the interest in these progressions.

Ex. 140   Symphony of Psalms p46   *Stravinsky*

Example 141 is another using only major triads and emphasizing contrary motion between the outer voices. The progression is as interesting as it is unusual, with chord roots on D, C-sharp, E-flat, C-natural, and back to D.

Ex. 141   Serenade: Sonnet   *Britten*

Roy Harris achieves a striking cadential effect by following four minor triads with two major triads, no two of which have the same interval between roots.

Ex. 142   American Ballads No. 1   *Harris*

The final example illustrating free relationships of chord quality is the conclusion of *Mathis der Maler*. To facilitate reading and playing, the example has been transposed up a half step and most of the octave doublings are omitted. It is noteworthy that this thoroughly modern work ends with a passage of eighteen measures using, except for two seventh chords, triads exclusively. Its effect stems from the relation between these triads and the forceful scoring for the full brass choir.

Ex. 143   Mathis der Maler p89   *Hindemith*

Though the emphasis up to this point has been upon the freedom of relationship in quality, this freedom, as has been mentioned before, extends also to root relationships. Whereas conventional music of the tonal period uses root movements predominantly in fourths and fifths, music of the modal period has root movements in seconds and thirds with almost equal frequency. In this, as in the use of the modes, contemporary composers have more in common with those of the sixteenth century than with their immediate predecessors. The relaxation of tonality, the use of modes and the free substitution of modes, the use of dissonance and freedom of root relationship—these factors are all inextricably interrelated.

Root Relationships

It cannot be claimed that contemporary composers have introduced anything new in the matter of root movements, since all possible movements occur in conventional music. It is rather in a more ready admission of movements in seconds and thirds, along with an occasional augmented fourth or diminished fifth, and in the association of these movements with unusual qualities and structures that twentieth century harmony achieves distinction. These root movements are illustrated with simple harmonic structures, but as with the previous phases of the investigation of harmonic progression, they are equally valid for more complicated sonorities.

Root movements, in seconds are used exclusively in Example 144 up to the highly conventional cadence formula.

Ex. 144   Symphony No. 4 p48   *Sibelius*

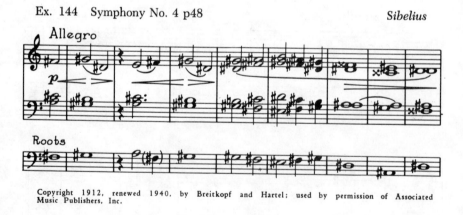

Avoiding traditional cadence formulas, Hindemith uses root movements in seconds, a minor followed by a major, for the final cadence of

the first movement in his symphony *Mathis der Maler*. Note the expanding motion of the moving parts.

Ex. 145   Mathis der Maler p32   *Hindemith*

Example 146 opens with major triads on consecutive descending scale degrees coupled with an ascending bass line and contracting outer voices. The cadence progression, also with a root relationship of a second, sounds like a deceptive cadence in B minor.

Ex. 146   Classical Symphony p15   *Prokofieff*

Example 147 utilizes a variety of root movements. Root relationships of perfect and diminished fifths, major and minor thirds, and ascending and descending major seconds occur in its five measures.

Ex. 147   Piano Concerto No. 3 p 32   *Bartok*

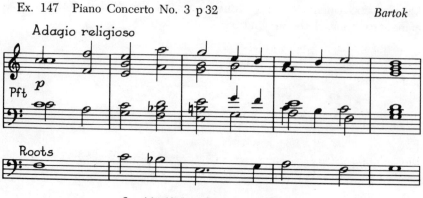

The beginning of the melody in Example 148 is an inversion of that in Example 147. In this setting root movements in thirds and fifths alternate until the final progression, which is an effective use of the augmented fourth relationship.

Ex. 148   Piano Concerto No. 3 p 32   *Bartok*

Parallelism

Parallelism other than between imperfect consonances and first inversions of triads, studiously avoided from the renaissance to the advent of impressionism, is a firmly established facet of contemporary harmonic technique. Pioneered by Debussy and the impressionists, it has virtually become their hallmark. Parallelism is no longer used with the abandon of its innovators, but it has played a vital role in freeing voice leading from arbitrary restrictions and in fostering broader concepts of tonality. Parallelism also tends to reduce the functional effect of harmony and to increase its coloristic value.

The principle of parallel movement applied to intervals formerly forbidden and to complete harmonies has many applications. One of the simplest is doubling of a melodic line with triads all in the same position illustrated in Example 149. These same harmonies could be used in a conventional manner by inverting some of them and observing traditional voice leading practices, but the effect would be quite different. Major and minor qualities are used, but diminished is avoided through the use of either B-natural or E-flat. Parallel fifths as well as triads result in every progression.

Ex. 149   Preludes Book II No. 10   *Debussy*

Ravel uses parallel triads with emphasis on the major quality to accompany an independent melody in Example 150.

Ex. 150   Piano Sonatine p2   *Ravel*

Modéré

Parallel seventh chords in first inversion with the fifths omitted and then in root position complete are used in Example 151. All of the notes are in D-flat major, so the type of chord varies as they move up the scale, and every diatonic seventh structure in major appears.

Ex. 151   The Firebird p40   *Stravinsky*

Parallel motion between ninth chords is a popular device of the impressionists and of dance band arrangers. Debussy uses them with roots a major third and minor second apart in Example 152.

Ex. 152   Pelleas and Melisande p14 *Debussy*

Permission for reprint granted by Durand & Cie., Paris, France, copyright owners: Elkan-Vogel Co., Inc., Philadelphia, Pa., agents.

All of the chords in Example 153 are ninths in the most usual spacing—with the root in the bass and the ninth in the soprano. The chord on A-natural has a neighboring chord effect as it comes between the D-flat and B-flat chords.

Ex. 153   Three Nocturnes: Fetes p20   *Debussy*

The use of parallel ninth chords is by no means restricted to impressionist and popular composers. Stravinsky uses them, but in a very different way.

Ex. 154   Petrouchka p57   *Stravinsky*

Parallel movement of triads in conjunction with other notes is used by Hindemith. The F and G in the treble clef are added sixths, and the C in measure 3 has the effect of a suspension.

Ex. 155   Mathis der Maler p62   *Hindemith*

Parallelism is not a characteristic feature of Schoenberg's style, but parallel seventh chords occur in Example 156, included to show the diversified application of the principle. The chords are broken and the right hand part is independent of the seventh chord structure, but the parallel motion is obvious.

Ex. 156   Three Piano Pieces Op. 11 No. 2   *Schoenberg*

The strong influence of parallel progression on contemporary music is evident, though in current practice its use tends to be more imaginative and subtle than when parallelism itself was sufficiently novel to create interest.

The complete harmonic resources of Mozart and Beethoven considered in terms of isolated chord structures and individual root movements can be summed up in a page or two, but a systematic study of these limited materials proves ample for extended courses in traditional harmony. A comparably definitive study of contemporary harmony would require volumes. The foregoing, however, outlines the main streams of harmonic development during this century and lays a foundation for writing and understanding recent harmonic procedures. Each style and method should be explored in composition exercises. The harmonic processes appropriate to a composer's mode of expression are instinctively incorporated in his musical language, and as resources are assimilated his distinctive creative personality emerges.

Suggested Assignments

1. Locate and describe examples of parallelism in Debussy's *Preludes for Piano.*

2. Find triads in the "Sonnet" from Britten's *Serenade for Tenor, Horn, and Strings,* and determine the mode(s) if any in which each is diatonic. (See Example 138)

3. Analyze the root relationships in the third movement of Prokofieff's *Classical Symphony.*

4. Write appropriate modal settings for the modal melodies previously composed.

5. Provide accompaniments with freely derived qualities and varied root relationships for original or assigned melodies.

6. Make settings for the best melodies written as synthetic scale and expanded tonality assignments. When the melodic line implies distinctive chord structures, reflect the implication in the harmony. In harmonizing synthetic scale melodies, consider the possibility of deriving the melody and the harmony from the same scale.

7. Write an exercise in which parallel progressions predominate.

8. Starting from the isolated chord structures written as assignments for Chapter V, write effective resolutions and progressions of three or four chords ending with a satisfactory cadence, though not necessarily a triad. Strive for a consistent, homogeneous effect within each progression and for variety between progressions.

CHAPTER VII

Rhythm and Meter

Two basic elements of music—melody and harmony—have been examined. The third and next to be considered is rhythm. Rhythmic developments during this century have kept pace with those in melody and harmony. Twentieth century rhythmic concepts, as well as those in other areas, are an outgrowth of immediate prior practice and show influences of earlier musical styles as well.

Rhythm, like melody and harmony, is now freer and more varied than in the past. Among the conventions which inhibited rhythmic flexibility during the two previous centuries were constant metric patterns, regularly spaced bar lines, and four-measure phrases. Composers in revolt against these conventions became the rhythmic innovators of the present century. Though time signatures, bar lines, metric accents, and four-measure phrases are not defunct, their tyrannical domination of rhythmic organization has been broken. Fresh possibilities have been added to those inherited from our predecessors, and complete freedom from arbitrary restrictions is taken for granted. Cataloging all the new rhythmic devices is not feasible. A survey of the more fruitful trends will suffice as an introduction to twentieth century rhythm.

Nonaccentual Rhythms

Traditionally, beats immediately following bar lines are stressed. Secondary stresses occur within longer measures, e.g., on 3 of 4/4 measures. Generations of composers wrote music applying these principles; performers are still trained to observe them; and listeners are expected to perceive their operation. Though a wealth of music has been created embodying this rhythmic concept, its limitations are obvious.

One way to circumvent such limitations is to preserve bar lines solely as a convenience of notation, disregarding in composition and performance any metric or accentual implications they formerly had. The effect is to create music without audible bar lines. This idea is not new. It existed in plain chant and in the vocal music of the sixteenth century. Renewed interest in sixteenth century vocal polyphony has done much to revive it.

In the absence of metric accents, notes which are approached by leap, prolonged, or embellished become focal points. Functionally they correspond to metric stresses, but being independent of the meter they may fall any place in the measure. They are most effective when their freedom from metric regulation is exercised.

The metric divisions defined by bar lines in Example 157 cannot be detected in the sound. Ties across bar lines obliterate the metric accents and produce a subtle, free-flowing rhythm in which the six-measure phrases marked by the composer sound neither irregular nor extended.

Ex. 157   Symphony No. 3 p3   *Harris*

Example 158 illustrates the same type of rhythmic feeling, though the stresses start to coincide with the bar lines at the end. Often, as in this example, free-flowing, nonaccentual passages of short duration lead directly into metrically oriented patterns. Internal repetitions create the effect of extensions, but phrase divisions are not clearly defined.

Ex. 158   Symphony No. 3 p46   *Schuman*

Ties over the bar line are found frequently in melodies of this sort. This is one way of eliminating the effect of the bar and its implied accent. Phrasing marks assume an added importance in passages with non-accentual rhythm, because the performers are playing in a manner contrary to their conditioning.

Shifted Accents

The previous two examples achieve flexibility of rhythm by eliminating or camouflaging the usual rhythmic accents. Another way to achieve the effect of rhythmic flexibility is to accent normally unaccented portions of the measure. This can be done with symbols or by heavier writing and/or scoring in the places to be accented.

Walton marks accents on certain second and third beats in Example 159 to shift the stresses from their normal position in the measure.

Ex. 159   Symphony p106   *Walton*

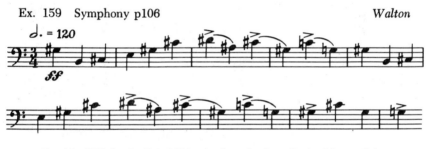

Sometimes an accent shift is associated with a rhythmic or melodic pattern which does not conform to the metric divisions, as in Example 160.

Ex. 160   Symphony No. 1 p96   *Milhaud*

Accents may be shifted fractions of a beat as well as full beats. Example 161 illustrates this possibility.

Ex. 161   The Firebird p24   *Stravinsky*

Accents which shift in relation to the beat but coincide with the high points in the line provide an intricate rhythm in Example 162.

Ex. 162   The Rite of Spring p30   *Stravinsky*

The accented beginning of the descending figure in Example 163 is shifted a sixteenth later in each repetition.

Ex. 163   Symphony No. 3 p131   *Copland*

Note groupings foreign to the meter are not always marked by accents. Unaccented groupings of this sort are indicated by phrasing marks or by beams joining notes within a group. Since phrasing marks also indicate bowing in string music, Schoenberg uses beams in Example 164

to show groupings which do not correspond to normal metrical divisions.

Ex. 164   String Quartet No. 4 p59   *Schoenberg*

Bowing is not a factor in the example from the Bartok piano piece, but he beams together groups of sixteenth notes which shift position in relation to the beat. Other interpretations are possible, but the notation suggests that each group is to be played in the same way. This in effect shifts the location of the accents in reference to the notated beats and bar lines, which would not be perceived by listeners.

Ex. 165   Mikrokosmos Vol. VI No. 146   *Bartok*

Walton makes extensive and imaginative use of rhythmic shifts. Example 166 is particularly interesting. The accents do not comply with any metric division or consistent pattern, and they occur on every beat and half beat of the measure.

Ex. 166   Belshazzar's Feast p70   *Walton*

Roy Harris capitalizes on the fact that 3/2 and 6/4 meters have the same number of quarter notes but different secondary accents to write a theme with an unusual rhythmic effect. Each measure fits into one pattern or the other, but mixing them adds a unique touch. With the unexpected accents, the five-measure phrase goes unnoticed in Example 167.

Ex. 167   Symphony No. 3 p56   *Harris*

Asymmetric Divisions

Momentarily displaced metric accents, which often produce asymmetric rhythmic units, are illustrated in the previous examples. An asymmetric division of measures sometimes is consistent throughout a composition or extended section. Example 168 has measures of eight eighth notes grouped 3-3-2 as indicated by the signature. This division is used in the piece without exception.

Ex. 168   Mikrokosmos Vol. VI No. 153   *Bartok*

Bartok indicates groupings of 4-2-3 for measures of nine eighth
notes in Example 169. This division is consistent for the entire first part
of the movement from which the example is taken.

Ex. 169   String Quartet No. 5 p31   *Bartok*

In the *Trio* of the same movement, Bartok adds an eighth note to
the measure, for a total of ten, which he also divides asymmetrically.

Ex. 170   String Quartet No. 5 p35   *Bartok*

Asymmetric Meters

Not only does Example 170 have an asymmetric division of the
measure, but it contains a number of eighth notes which cannot be ac-

comodated in any conventional meter. A more usual division of ten eighth notes into five groups of two would be indicated by a signature of 5/4. Asymmetric meters like 5/4 represent still another means for achieving rhythmic variety.

Five/four meter was one of the first asymmetric meters to be used, and it still is one of the most favored. It may be divided either three and two or two and three. Ravel uses the former consistently in Example 171 and indicates the division within the measure by a dotted bar line.

Ex. 171   Daphnis & Chloe p87   *Ravel*

Piston uses a 7/8 meter in his *Divertimento* with accents placed to suggest a division of 2-3-2.

Ex. 172   Divertimento p1   *Piston*

The same meter divides 2-2-3 or 4-3 in the following Bartok example.

Ex. 173   Mikrokosmos Vol. III No. 82   *Bartok*

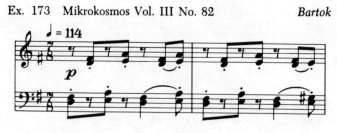

Stravinsky divides nine eighths asymmetrically 4-5 and then 5-4. Example 174 gives the signatures as they appear in the score.

Ex. 174   The Rite of Spring p31   *Stravinsky*

Changing Meters

Up to this point the examples have illustrated various ways of achieving rhythmic variety within constant measures. Measures of varied lengths and meters are another source of variety. These require changing time signatures, a trademark of twentieth century rhythm.

With changing meters, bar lines exercise their traditional functions, but they are no longer bound to fixed positions. They move fluidly to delineate rhythmic patterns and to suggest rhythmic stresses. Instead of fitting the music to the measures, the measures are fitted to the music. Composers are not reluctant to change time signatures as often as necessary to notate precisely irregular and asymmetric musical ideas. These are prevalent in contemporary music, and practically every score provides examples of changing meters. Time signature changes are an added hazard for players and conductors but not for composers, who have long been writing them with obvious relish.

Time changes may be but are not necessarily associated with complexity. Example 175 is from a simple piece for children.

Ex. 175   Piano Pieces for Children Vol. II No. 30   *Bartok*

The Rite of Spring, written more than half a century ago, makes extensive use of meter changes. Some are relatively simple, like Example 176. Others, like Example 177, are extremely complex.

Ex. 176   The Rite of Spring p101   *Stravinsky*

Ex. 177   The Rite of Spring p112   *Stravinsky*

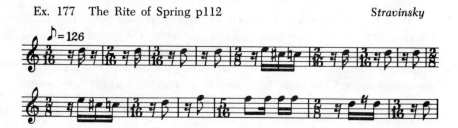

Additional examples of changing meter can be found in almost any contemporary work.

Five basic ways in which contemporary composers have expanded their rhythmic resources have been examined:

1. Through the use of nonaccentual rhythms
2. By shifting accents in relation to the beat and bar line
3. By asymmetric division of measures
4. Through the use of asymmetric meters
5. By changing meters

All of them tend to eliminate stereotyped rhythmic patterns and phrase structures.

Of the five ways listed above in which rhythmic resources have been expanded, all but the first figure in the next example.

Ex. 178   El Salon Mexico p1   *Copland*

Contemporary rhythmic resources embrace every duration and relationship that can be conceived, notated, and executed, including several possibilities infinitely more involved than those discussed here.
Among them are the highly personal and esoteric rhythmic procedures
of Olivier Messiaen elucidated in his book *The Technique of my Musical
Language**. Other composers and theorists currently are devising means
of serializing durations in ways related to and in some cases derived
from the twelve-tone system previously applied to pitches. Also, the new
electronic mediums are producing unprecedented rhythmic phenomena
both by design and by chance. These most recent rhythmic developments
are not sufficiently crystallized or widely enough disseminated to war-
rant inclusion at this time in a survey of contemporary techniques, though
they will have to be reckoned with in the not too distant future.

Practical young composers are well advised to use rhythmic devices which will intrigue but not discourage potential performers. Excessively intricate rhythms are an insurmountable barrier to the less experienced players who are more generally available. Besides, some of the
most effective rhythms are those which make only minor but striking
departures from convention.

Suggested Assignments

1. Locate and copy an example of twentieth century music (excluding
   works cited in this chapter) illustrating each of the five categories
   of rhythm discussed. Analyze the phrase structures.

2. Write a paper describing the rhythmic procedures in a contemporary
   work you have played or sung with special reference to the five
   categories listed.

---

*Translated by John Satterfield. Alphonse Leduc et Cie, Paris, 1944 and 1956.

3. Write a melody with nonaccentual rhythm similar in style to Examples 157 and 158.

4. Write an exercise in which accents shift in relation to the bar lines and/or beats.

5. Write an exercise in an asymmetric meter or with an asymmetric division of the measures.

6. Write an exercise in which change of meter is exploited as a characteristic feature.

7. Analyze the phrase structures of your exercises and compare them with the examples in the chapter.

8. Compose a short piece using characteristic contemporary rhythmic devices.

CHAPTER VIII

Tonality

When the elements of music explored in previous chapters—melody, harmony, and rhythm—are set in motion, tonality ordinarily results. While the implications of tonality are generally understood, a specific definition which embraces all contemporary usage of the term is difficult. Key, as used in the major-minor period, is not sufficiently broad to encompass the different aspects of tonality in current musical practice. Key usually implies (1) the use of a limited number of notes from a fixed pattern (a major or minor scale) as the basic source of material, (2) the admission of other notes in the texture only as auxiliaries with special restrictions, and (3) the assignment of definite functions to certain harmonic elements, e.g., tonic and dominant. Whereas these restrictions customarily are observed in traditional major-minor music, tonality is possible without them. Tonality in the broader sense implies only the presence of a tonal center.

Tonal centers can be established and perceived without limiting the sources or functions of material. The tendency of one tone to emerge and assert itself as the tonal center or tonic is a phenomenon observable in music from a wide variety of styles and periods. Only when consciously avoided is this tendency absent, but there are many degrees of tonality between that of a strong major key and a barely discernible tonal center. Twentieth century practices have led to broader and freer concepts. Some of these have been examined in connection with melodic and harmonic materials.

The use of modes, exotic and synthetic scales, and expanded tonality, all weaken the bonds of conventional key feeling. In the same way

115

the use of dissonant harmonies, parallel progressions, change of mode, and freedom in root relationships and quality reduce the influence of the tonal center on harmonic resources. All these factors have contributed to the diminishing sense of tonality in recent music without necessarily destroying the feeling for the center itself. In much of the music written during this century there is a perceptible tonal center which, however weak by conventional standards, serves in some degree to orient the flow of the sounds. By retaining the tonic function an invalauble source of variety—modulation—is also preserved.

Tonality in contemporary music is not the well defined, dominating force it was in the major-minor period. It is, however, an important aspect of current practice. This chapter surveys some facets of tonality beyond those mentioned in previous chapters.

Free Relationships of Tonality

Before the advent of equal temperament and valves, music for many instruments was restricted, for practical reasons, to closely related keys. Even after more remote keys were accessible, their full potential was not realized immediately. Contemporary composers, unhampered by convention or mechanical imperfections, take full advantage of the foreign tonal relationships available in addition to using all those common in earlier music. The use of foreign relationships is equally apparent in the modulations occuring within and between phrases and in transposition of themes in larger forms.

Remote tonal regions are traversed habitually in Hindemith's *Mathis der Maler*. The following excerpt from the second movement begins in C. The cadence at the end of the first phrase is on G-sharp. Though some notes are spelled enharmonically, the first chord of the next section is G-sharp minor. In two measures this leads back to the opening motive at the original pitch but with octave doublings. Aside from starting on the third beat of the measure and doublings, the beginning of this phrase is the same as the first. The end is changed to lead this time to C-sharp minor. Thus within ten measures the tonal center shifts from C to G-sharp, back to C, and to C-sharp.

Ex. 179   Mathis der Maler p33   *Hindemith*

The tonal relationships of the theme are characteristic of the movement as a whole. When the theme given above returns to complete a
ternary form, it begins a step lower in B-flat and ends in F-sharp major.
The movement which starts in C concludes, after a coda, in C-sharp
major.

Similar remote tonal relationships are exhibited in the first movement
of this same work. The design is that of sonata form except that the
order of the subordinate and closing themes is reversed in the recapitulation, but the key relationships are atypical. The beginnings of the principal, subordinate, and closing themes are shown in Example 180, first
as they appear in the exposition and then as they reappear in the recapitulation. The principal and subordinate themes are both a half step
higher in the recapitulation. The closing theme is a major third lower.

Ex. 180   Mathis der Maler, 1st Movement   *Hindemith*

The movement begins and ends with G as the tonal center. The statement of the principal theme, after an introduction, begins over G harmony. The return a half step higher commences with a D-flat major chord, partially spelled enharmonically. Beginning the recapitulation in a remote key violates a cardinal rule of classic form, but is quite acceptable by contemporary standards. Reversing the order of the subordinate and closing themes in the recapitulation and transposing the subordinate theme up a half step brings this theme back to the tonality of the opening, G, in which the movement ends.

After a tonally ambiguous introduction, the final movement proper of *Mathis der Maler* begins in C-sharp minor. This movement concludes on a D-flat major triad. The final chord can be explained as the major form of the tonic spelled enharmonically. This is much closer to a conventional relationship than that which exists between the first and last movements, the former having G as a tonal center, the latter C-sharp or D-flat.

These examples from Hindemith illustrate typical explorations of remote tonalities in recent music. The remote tonal relationships which were shunned by composers of the past have special appeal for composers of the present.

Shifted Tonality

Abrupt change of tonality is a mannerism of certain Soviet composers, and this device has sufficient currency in twentieth century music generally to justify its consideration. Related to modulation in traditional music, shifted tonality contrasts with conventional modulation in three basic respects. Where conventional modulations are prepared with common material and proceed smoothly to related keys, contemporary shifts in tonality are unprepared, precipitate, and typically to distant tonal regions.

These procedures are foreshadowed somewhat in the free relationships of quality found in harmonic progressions, but free quality relationships may orbit a single tonal center. Shifted tonality implies a sudden displacement of the old center by a new one. Since the surprise element is critical, the device is most effective when the harmonic materials are unsophisticated and both tonalities are fairly obvious. As a rule the new key appears unexpectedly at a strategic point in the phrase struc-‘ture.

The unanticipated tonal shifts in Example 181 are from D to A-flat and then to G.

Ex. 181   Classical Symphony p17   *Prokofieff*

Example 182 has a similar shift of tonality but returns to the original center at the end.

Ex. 182   Peter and the Wolf p1   *Prokofieff*

Copyright 1942 by Hawkes & Son (London), Ltd.

Shostakovich is another Soviet composer in whose music examples of shifted tonality abound. Examples 183 and 184, taken from his *Fifth Symphony,* use some chromatic material before the actual shift, but the effect is only slightly diminished.

Ex. 183   Symphony No. 5 p58   *Shostakovich*

Ex. 184   Symphony No. 5 p66   *Shostakovich*

Used judiciously, tonal shifts are an effective adjunct to compositional resources. Used excessively, they become an annoying mannerism.

Dual Modality

Conventional music in minor keys customarily makes use of notes from different forms of the minor scales. Even in the baroque and classic periods the use of the raised and lowered sixth and seventh degrees of the minor scale led to cross relations and occasionally to double inflections. With the use of the *Picardy Third*, the mode changed from minor to major. These practices have contemporary counterparts.

The possibility of using alternately material from various modes with the same tonic was explored somewhat in connection with harmonic progression. Carried further this leads to the use of two modes with the same tonic or two forms of the same chord simultaneously. This will be called *dual modality*. Dual modality is most apparent when two inflexions of the same note occur together or in close juxtaposition. Though theoretically possible with the ecclesiastical modes, dual modality is common only between major and minor.

Oscillation between major and minor thirds in sustained harmony is a characteristic feature of Example 185. It occurs in measures 2, 4, 6, 8, and 9. The minor third of the D-flat chord is spelled enharmonically, as is the minor seventh.

Ex. 185   Symphony No. 3 p4   *Harris*

Example 186 illustrates the use of dual modality to produce consistent cross relations between sonorities containing either B-flat or B-natural.

Ex. 186   Piano Sonata p5   *Copland*

Example 187, with a melody entirely in A minor and an accompaniment essentially in A major, illustrates effectively the use of dual modality between these two elements.

Ex. 187   String Quartet No. 2 p17   *Bartok*

A more extended and systematic use of dual modality is illustrated in Example 188. The right hand draws its material exclusively from C minor, the left from C major to the first cadence. From there to the fifth measure from the end the mode in each hand is reversed.

Ex. 188   Mikrokosmos Vol. II No. 59   *Bartok*

Example 189 shows a less obvious dual modality, but the major-minor implication is apparent in the B harmony of measure 1 and in the G harmony of measures 3 and 4.

Ex. 189   Symphony in Three Movements p27   *Stravinsky*

Dual modality is a specialized effect with limited usage, but one capable of providing delightfully pungent sounds with resources not far removed from tradition.

Polytonality

It is but a short step from the use of two modes to the use of two tonalities. This is known as *polytonality*. Strictly speaking, *bitonality* would be a more accurate designation, since more than two tonal centers at the same time are rare, but polytonality is the more prevalent term.

Revolutionary as the idea of polytonality may seem, it is not unprecedented. Incipient polytonality can be detected in strongly tonal music. For example, the answer and countersubject in the exposition of a real fugue may suggest different keys briefly when played separately even though they are perceived as being in the same key when played together. The countersubject by itself may continue to imply the tonic key (of the subject) until distinctive material of the new key such as its leading tone is introduced. The answer enters meanwhile directly in the dominant key. This is not conceived as a polytonal effect. It results spontaneously from the preponderance of common tones between the two keys. In contrast with this are the calculated exploitations of remote polytonal relationships in modern music.

Dissonant harmony and counterpoint frequently have polytonal implications, but the term is usually reserved for passages in which two or more tonal centers are rather clearly apparent. In this respect it should be noted they often are more obvious to the eye than to the ear. Listeners are perfectly capable of appreciating the effect even when they are not able to isolate the various keynotes. For polytonality to be consciously perceived, the two keys must be relatively pure and adequately separated in register and timbre.

Milhaud was an early exponent of polytonality, and it figures prominently in his works. The polytonal effect in Example 190 is heightened by the imitation and the remoteness of the relationship.

Ex. 190   Suite Francaise p15   *Milhaud*

The polytonality in Britten's setting of *The Ash Grove* is particularly interesting because of the shift of tonal center in the counterpoint on the repetition of the melody. Against the folk song in F, the added part is first in B-flat and then in D-flat, except for the one G-natural.

Ex. 191   Folk Songs of the British Isles Vol. 1 No. 6   *Britten*

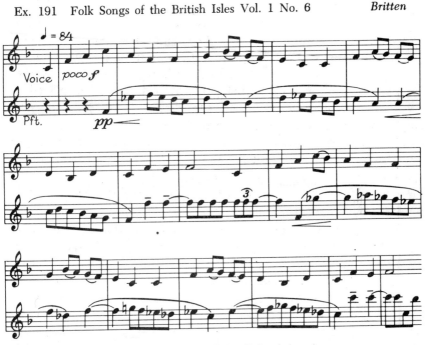

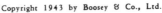

Polytonal implications are of course possible between more than two voices. Of the four voices in Example 192, the upper pair suggests an E tonality and the mirroring lower pair an F-sharp tonality, both in minor modes.

Ex. 192   String Quartet No. 2 p48   *Bartok*

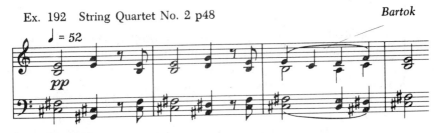

A more typical and obvious polytonal passage is given in Example 193. The black key-white key relationship shown is a favorite in piano music.

Ex. 193   Violin Sonata No. 2 p14   *Milhaud*

In the foregoing examples each tonality was founded on a conventional scale. This is usual, but other scales may figure in polytonal textures. Example 194 is based on the two whole tone scales used in a manner which produces perpetual melodic doubling at the minor third. All such melodic doublings at constant intervals have polytonal implications. (See Chapter IV).

Ex. 194   Mikrokosmos Vol. V No. 136   *Bartok*

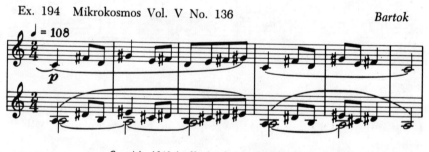

Polytonality has limitless applications covering a wide range of dissonance and complexity. It can be used in two part counterpoint and in massive chords; between closely related and foreign keys. Though only two-key polytonality is illustrated, combinations of three and more keys are not unknown.

The novelty of polytonality can no longer be counted on to sustain interest as it did earlier in the century. Obvious and systematic displays of polytonality are uncommon in mid-century music. It is a useful concept which has been integrated with other resources, and its influence is felt in many passages.

Pandiatonicism

Pandiatonicism is a natural reaction to the excessive chromaticism in late romantic and contemporary music. Pandiatonic music reverts to the diatonic scale for its source material. Only the absence of characteristic harmonic and melodic functions sets it apart from conventional non-chromatic music. Traditional tonal progressions and cadence formulas are foreign to the style. The following passage is typical.

Ex. 195   Appalachian Spring p51   *Copland*

Copyright 1945 by Hawkes & Son (London), Ltd.

Listeners are quickly satiated with the sounds of pandiatonicism, but sparing use of its quaint flavor is appealing.

Suggested Assignments

1. Establish a tonality, make a remote modulation, and return to the original center within a continuous musical idea.
2. Write an exercise in which the repetition of a fragment in a remote tonality is an essential feature.
3. Compose a short piece employing shifting tonality characteristically.
4. Provide an appropriate accompaniment in the parallel major for an original minor melody.
5. Write a polytonal two part counterpoint exercise.
6. Write a passage for piano featuring black key-white key polytonality.
7. Exploit the principle of pandiatonicism in a brief exercise.
8. Find examples of twentieth century music illustrating several of the procedures described in the preceding assignments. The sources of the examples in the text provide clues to where each may be found.

CHAPTER IX

Cadences

Since cadences in the periods immediately preceding our own were constructed from a limited number of stereotyped formulas, expansion of the cadence concept in the present century was inevitable. However, certain considerations peculiar to cadence points restrain the renunciation of traditional patterns. Listeners thoroughly conditioned to the perfect authentic cadence are disturbed by radical departures from its preconceived configurations. Furthermore, the dissonant harmonies which dominate contemporary music and serve admirably in building tension within phrases are deficient in the repose quality required to conclude them. For these reasons cadences in contemporary idioms pose special problems. Composers in their quest for fresh cadential materials seek tonal combinations which will be perceived as cadences, because the aural perception of cadences is essential to the comprehension of music, especially in the matter of form.

Representative contemporary cadence procedures are illustrated. For the sake of uniformity the examples have been selected from final cadences ending works or movements, but the same types are found within movements providing both complete and incomplete cadence functions. The distinctions between complete and incomplete cadences formerly made on the basis of chord structures and progressions are no longer valid. Cadential resources are too varied to be classified on that basis, but they do not introduce chord structures or progressions that have not been studied previously. Rather, they show these materials serving cadential functions. Since cadences are completely meaningful only in connection with the entire musical idea they bring to a close, it is suggested that the passages preceding the examples be examined whenever possible.

Modified Dominants

In conventional music the formula for a complete cadence consists ordinarily of a progression from dominant to tonic. Not only does the dominant have a specified structure and stand in a fixed relationship to the tonic, but the movement of the individual voices is regulated by tradition. The only facet of this formula honored consistently by contemporary composers is the progression of an active sound to a less active or repose sound, and even this has its exceptions. The contemporary cadences which have the most in common with convention are those which keep the dominant-tonic function intact and modify only the structure of the dominant and/or its relationship to the tonic.

Example 196 has the traditional fifth relationship between the dominant and tonic and differs from tradition only in the use of the minor dominant and the upward resolution of its seventh. The diverging chromatic lines contribute to the cadential effect. The D-sharp and F-natural in the chromatic lines are heard as chromatic passing tones against the D-natural and F-sharp of the chord.

Ex. 196   Piano Concerto No. 3 p91   *Bartok*

The fifth relationship is preserved, but the structure of the dominant in Example 197 represents a further departure from convention.

Ex. 197   Concerto for Orchestra p28   *Bartok*

The interval of a perfect fifth on the leading tone provides the dominant function in Example 198.

Ex. 198   Symphony No. 3 p103   *Harris*

The final E major of Example 199 is preceded by a sonority which sounds like a seventh chord on D with an unresolved 4-3 suspension. The minor implication of the imitation just before the cadence gives the effect of a picardy third.

Ex. 199   Piano Concerto No. 3 p48   *Bartok*

Typical dominant function is missing in Example 200 where the A-flat minor triad comes between the major tonic triad and the final tonic note, F.

Ex. 200   Symphony No. 1 p92   *Shostakovich*

Example 201 is curious in that the notes of the tonic are anticipated in the previous chords. The open fifth, which leaves the mode indeterminate, is a favored tonic structure.

Ex. 201   Symphony No. 1 p49   *Piston*

Modified Tonics

Notes beyond the normal triad can be added to the tonic without distorting it beyond recognition. Example 202 has the C tonic with an added sixth approached from an inverted seventh chord on B.

Ex. 202   Histoire du Soldat p6   *Stravinsky*

The final chord of Stravinsky's *Symphony in Three Movements* has an added sixth and an added second.

Ex. 203   Symphony in Three Movements p120   *Stravinsky*

The final sonority of Prokofieff's *Third Piano Concerto* contains all
the notes of the tonic and dominant triads of C major.

Ex. 204   Piano Concerto No. 3 p180   *Prokofieff*

Dual modality is carried over to the concluding tonic in Example
205, and both the major and minor thirds are present.

Ex. 205   Mikrokosmos Vol. IV No. 108   *Bartok*

The final sonority in *The Rite of Spring*, with its dissonant elements
and close spacing in a low register, has a percussive effect. This is a
decided departure from a traditional tonic triad, but it serves the purpose effectively for this particular work.

Ex. 206   The Rite of Spring p139   *Stravinsky*

The next step after the use of a percussive sonority for a tonic is the use of percussion instruments alone which Stravinsky does in the following example.

Ex. 207   Histoire du Soldat p 68   *Stravinsky*

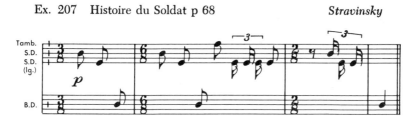

Linear Cadences

The motion of the individual voices is always of primary importance at cadence points. Some cadences are more the result of lines than of harmonies. This is necessarily the case when a composition ends with a single line, like *Petrouchka*. The dominant-tonic relationship is established between the C-sharp and the F-sharp in spite of the intervening D-sharp and C-natural.

Ex. 208 Petrouchka p156   *Stravinsky*

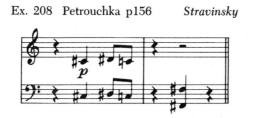

The diverging lines of Example 209 are reminiscent not only of Example 196 but of many prebaroque cadences. Contrary motion moving stepwise to the tonic is a venerable cadence device which has many present day applications.

Ex. 209   String Quartet No. 5 p92   *Bartok*

Contrary motion moving stepwise to the root and fifth of the tonic provides the essential ingredient for the cadence in Example 210. The penultimate harmony, being a major chord a half step above the tonic, illustrates a relationship which has been exploited frequently in contemporary cadences.

Ex. 210   Ludus Tonalis: Fuga Septima   *Hindemith*

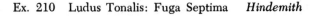

Noncadential Endings

Some compositions end without any approximation or reasonable facsimile of a traditional cadence. The active-repose elements or strong linear motion considered essential by conventional composers and most moderns are lacking. Endings of this sort—the word cadence hardly seems appropriate—are associated most often with music which is essentially atonal, and more particularly with that composed in the twelve-

tone technique as these are. Two examples from Schoenberg illustrate
this type of ending.

Ex. 211   String Quartet No. 4 p107   *Schoenberg*

The solo part in the following would seem to suggest B-flat as the
tonality, but this is not substantiated in the other parts. Eight of the
twelve possible notes, including two double inflections, are sounding at
the close of the movement.

Ex. 212   Violin Concerto p28   *Schoenberg*

In endings of this sort and in all cadences which tend to be ambiguous, tempo and dynamics assume added importance. Cadences which
otherwise might be unconvincing are made believable by changes in
tempo and dynamics or by a fermata. Repetition also helps to establish
cadential function. Observe the repetition in the top voice of both the
Schoenberg examples. Harmonic progressions, lines, rhythm, tempo, dynamics, and (in performance) phrasing are factors capable of contribu-

ting to cadential function. When some of these are obscure, others tend
to compensate.

In contemporary composition it is neither possible nor desirable to
establish rigid cadence formulas. A suitable cadence, one appropriate to
the style and medium and fulfilling the structural requirements, must be
devised for each cadence point in every work. It is admittedly more difficult than applying a ready made formula, but it is also more interesting
and more challenging. These models show some of the ways this challenge has been and may be met.

Suggested Assignments

1. Analyze the final cadences in several contemporary compositions for
   various mediums and classify them according to the headings in this
   chapter. Make new categories if you discover cadences that do not
   fit those given.

2. Re-examine the cadences written for previous assignments. Change
   any that can be improved by using devices explored in this chapter.

3. Write a short exercise ending with a cadence using a modified dominant and/or tonic.

4. Compose a two part piece ending with a linear cadence that does
   not suggest a conventional dominant.

CHAPTER X

Nonharmonic Materials

When harmonic material is limited exclusively to triads and seventh chords, the isolation of nonharmonic material is a simple process. Any tone which does not fit in an accepted harmonic structure is nonharmonic. Nonharmonic tones in this context are easily classified by the motion of the line in which they occur and their relationship to the prevailing harmony. Traditional harmony books deal exhaustively with the various categories of nonharmonic tones found in this type of music and with the restrictions customarily observed by the composers of the period. Formerly, nonharmonic tones with few exceptions moved by step between chord tones or resolved by step to chord tones. The terminology for the various types is not standardized, but the following descriptive designations generally will be understood: *passing tones, neighboring tones or auxiliaries, suspensions, retardations, anticipations, free anticipations or escape tones, appoggiaturas, changing tones,* and *pedal points.* By whatever name they are known, all the nonharmonic procedures of earlier periods are still available.

Unlike the many aspects of conventional technique which have fallen into disuse, nonharmonic materials are as vital today as ever. The melodic patterns and relationships suggested by the conventional classifications occur regularly in recent music, but the sharp dividing line between nonharmonic and harmonic has disappeared, along with the restrictions. When every conceivable dissonance is permissible as a harmonic element, no clear distinction is possible. In contemporary music, notes are perceived as nonharmonic when they have a close affinity with one of the conventional categories or when they occur in relatively uncomplicated textures. Lacking these prerequisites, notes tend to be assimilated in the harmonic or contrapuntal fabric even though they may be dissonant. Traditional theory justifies many sounds on the basis of nonharmonic function that otherwise would have been unacceptable. Obviously, such justifications no longer are necessary, but the materials remain to be used and listeners are conditioned to accept and expect them.

In surveying nonharmonic materials in twentieth century music, no attempt has been made to recapitulate those practices covered in traditional theory or those which represent only slight modifications. The types considered are representative rather than exhaustive, but they illustrate current attitudes toward several conventional nonharmonic procedures.

The principle in conventional theory of resolving nonharmonic tones by step has no place in contemporary practice. Dissonances are left by leap freely. In the simple harmony of Example 213, the B-flat is perceived as nonharmonic. Because of its short duration and unaccented position in the measure, it does not establish itself as a chord member, yet it is left by leap consistently.

Ex. 213   Belshazzar's Feast p2   *Walton*

Against a more complicated harmonic background, dissonant tones are left with equal freedom in Example 214. While the B and A-sharp are sustained, the bass moves up chromatically from G and the notes on the beat in the top line progress down chromatically from E-sharp. The

Ex. 214   Mikrokosmos Vol. VI No. 147   *Bartok*

notes interposed between those of the descending chromatic scale are approached and left with complete freedom though they are dissonant and outside the pattern of the converging chromatic scales.

Passing tones, too, are treated with added freedom in recent times. Example 215 from early in the century has a scale in sixths in conjunction with seventh chord progressions. The scale motion produces double and single passing tones, as well as chord tones, and clusters result when the passing tones come between chord tones. Unlike conventional passing tones, which generally came between harmonies and were of shorter duration, these move in the same rhythm as the chords.

Ex. 215   The Firebird p77   *Stravinsky*

Conventional passing tones normally were unrepeated and moved without interruption to chord tones. Example 216 has double passing tones which not only are reiterated and form clusters with the chord tones but which are separated by rests from their resolution.

Ex. 216   Te Deum p26   *Kodaly*

In spite of the somewhat greater dissonance the progressions in Example 217 are the direct descendants of conventional passing chords. Observe the stepwise voice leading in both similar and contrary motion.

Ex. 217   Mathis der Maler p7   *Hindemith*

Complete passing chords also occur in contemporary music while the prevailing harmony is sustained or reiterated, as in Example 218.

Ex. 218   Petrouchka p44   *Stravinsky*

The middle line of Example 219 has double and triple contemporary counterparts of unprepared chromatic lower neighboring tones.

Ex. 219   Divertimento p10   *Piston*

Example 220 has somewhat the effect of neighboring tones, though not all of them resolve stepwise. It also is reminiscent of white key-black key polytonality.

Ex. 220   Ludus Tonalis: Interludium p38   *Hindemith*

The structure of an unresolved 4-3 suspension on various pitches persists without interruption for the duration of a short piano piece by William Schuman. The beginning and the end, with the eventual resolution, are shown in Example 221.

Ex. 221   Three Score Set No. 1   *Schuman*

Pedal points and ostinato figures in conventional music normally begin and end as consonances, but not necessarily in current styles. The shift in tonality of the upper voices is not reflected in the bass of Example 222.

Ex. 222   Symphony No. 9 p8   *Shostakovich*

The pedal note D in Example 223 is introduced as a consonance, but it too is left momentarily after a dissonance. Also, the harmonies above the pedal point range further afield than is possible with the key restrictions prevalent in previous periods.

Ex. 223   Belshazzar's Feast p3   *Walton*

Example 224 shows an inverted pedal introduced and left as a dissonance and in a remote relationship to the sonorities that come under it.

Ex. 224   Mathis der Maler p37   *Hindemith*

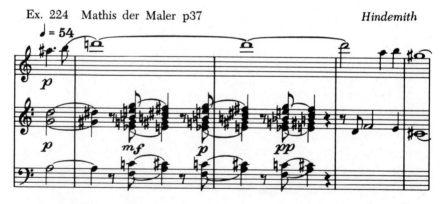

Pedal points in contemporary music frequently have a rhythmic value. The rhythm may be assigned to a single pitch, or to more than one as in Example 225. This double pedal point with a two-measure rhythmic pattern persists for twenty-eight measures at the beginning of Walton's *Symphony*. Other notes are substituted for the F at that point, but the rhythmic pattern and the B-flat continue as elements of a pedal for thirty-nine measures more.

Ex. 225   Symphony p1   *Walton*

Repeated patterns of more than two notes are considered under OSTINATO in Chapter XI.

The foregoing examples suffice to demonstrate that contemporary composers, though completely uninhibited in their use of dissonance, still find many uses for material with a recognizable relationship to traditional nonharmonic patterns. Current idioms do not discard resources but rather use them with greater abandon.

Suggested Assignments

1. Find examples of unconventional nonharmonic tones in contemporary music. Analyze and classify them.

2. Review exercises written for previous assignments to see if they can be made more interesting through more imaginative use of nonharmonic materials.

3. Write an exercise with a relatively simple harmonic background and a melody which has dissonances approached and left by leap.

4. Employ passing tones or passing chords in an unconventional manner in an exercise.

5. Write an effective harmonic progression over or under a pedal tone.

6. Write a two part exercise in which dissonances between the voices are resolved in an unconventional manner.

CHAPTER **XI**

Motivation of Harmony

In homophonic music various means of sustaining the sound of chords and motivating them rhythmically are necessary. These requirements were satisfied during the classic and romantic periods by repeated chords and sundry arpeggio figurations, including *Alberti bass*. Basic types of harmonic motivation were modified and embellished for variety, and contrapuntal procedures were always available as an antidote for the monotony of a strict homophonic style. The search for new ways to motivate harmony seems not to have been a primary concern in the past, but nowadays composers are reluctant to employ stereotyped formulas in harmonic motivation or any other function. This no doubt is partially responsible for the fact that living composers on the whole have been less prolific than their predecessors. The pursuit of total originality is a time consuming and sometimes unrewarding occupation, so vestiges of the old accompaniment patterns persist. Creative imagination functions in adapting and applying them to twentieth century sonorities, progressions, and rhythms. The following examples are typical.

Motivation of New Harmonic Resources

The application of old procedures to new harmonic resources provides a simple solution to the problem of harmonic motivation. Except that it does not outline a triad, the accompaniment figure in Example 226 could have come right out of Mozart or Haydn. The harmonic implication and the relationship between the melody and accompaniment place it well within the present century.

Ex. 226   Twenty-four Preludes No. 9   *Shostakovich*

The accompaniment figure in Example 227 is an obvious descendant of Alberti bass. The arpeggiation of chords in fourths, alternately in root position and first inversion, contributes to the fresh sound as do the progressions.

Ex. 227   Mikrokosmos Vol. V No. 125   *Bartok*

Repeated chords with unconventional structures also serve as accompaniment figures in recent music.

Ex. 228   Mikrokosmos Vol. VI No. 146   *Bartok*

The accompaniment in Example 229 can be analyzed either as an open fifth with neighboring tones or as a rapid alternation of fifths and thirds, but it is apt to be heard as a rhythmically animated sonority consisting of all four notes, E, F-sharp, A, and B.

Ex. 229   Piano Concerto No. 3 p1   *Bartok*

The affinity between the accompaniment in Example 230 and some found in Chopin is apparent at a glance. A closer examination reveals the source of its distinctive contemporary flavor in the more complex chord outlines.

Ex. 230   Piano Concerto No. 3 p36   *Prokofieff*

Example 231 illustrates a relatively new manner of motivating a harmonic sound. In the example it is possible to detect elements of imitation, inversion, and a polychord, but the total effect is that of an animated A major triad with a major seventh.

Ex. 231 Symphony No. 3 p23   *Harris*

Real polychords are animated in contrary motion with a rhythm of three against four in Example 232 for the greatest departure from convention yet illustrated in accompaniment figures.

Ex. 232   Violin Sonata p6   *Bloch*

Contemporary Rhythm in Harmonic Motivation

Most of the rhythmic features of contemporary music discussed in Chapter VII have applications in the motivation of harmonies. Example 233 illustrates the use of shifted accents with a repeated polychord which serves as a harmonic background. The chord is scored for strings with the accents, which occur irregularly, reinforced by horns.

Ex. 233   The Rite of Spring p11   *Stravinsky*

Asymmetric division of a measure containing 9 eighth notes is exploited in the accompaniment figure of Example 234.

Ex. 234   Mikrokosmos Vol. VI No. 148   *Bartok*

Example 235 is an accompaniment in an asymmetric meter, 5/4.

Ex. 235   Daphnis and Chloe p76   *Ravel*

Changing time signatures are basic to the harmonic motivation in the following example.

Ex. 236   Appalachian Spring p20   Copland

Accompaniment patterns are found exploiting the characteristic features of every type of contemporary rhythm except nonaccentual, to which they are by nature foreign.

Ostinato

Though the earliest use of ostinato dates back several centuries, the popularity of this device in the twentieth century is unprecedented. Because it has been used so extensively in recent times, the basic idea of ostinato has been subjected to many modifications, several of which are illustrated.

The first example, however, is close to the original concept of a melodic phrase repeated perpetually in a composition or passage. The C major scale ostinato in Example 237 continues without interruption for 33 measures. Unusual by conventional standards is the 4 1/2 measure length of the repeated pattern.

Ex. 237   Octet p32   *Stravinsky*

More regular in length but less usual in line is the ostinato, derived from the introduction, which sounds throughout most of the coda to the third movement of *Mathis der Maler.*

Ex. 238   Mathis der Maler p83   *Hindemith*

The bass of Example 239 is a three beat ostinato which shifts position in relation to the four beat measure. The irregular spacing of the punctuating chords is independent of the ostinato figure.

Ex. 239   Symphony in Three Movements p8   *Stravinsky*

The ostinato in Example 240 consists of complete triads with contrary motion between the bass and the upper parts. After two literal repetitions, rhythmic variations are introduced. The fifth measure modifies the ostinato pattern and leads to another one with full triads in contrary motion on each staff. This same process is repeated with subsequent phrases. The ostinato, which is in the orchestra, provides a harmonic background for the lines of the chorus.

Ex. 240   Merry Mount p250   *Hanson*

A more dissonant harmonic ostinato is illustrated in Example 241. The top line is vocal, the rest are in the orchestra. All five lines continue as an ostinato as other free vocal lines enter in the complete passage.

Ex. 241   The Medium p23   *Menotti*

An ostinato with imitation at the octave serves as accompaniment to a free melody in Example 242. The dotted bar line in the imitating part is shown as it appears in the score.

Ex. 242   String Quartet No. 5 p11   *Bartok*

Besides a double pedal point, there is an ostinato with rhythmically varied imitation at the octave in Example 243. This ostinato, like those in Examples 240 and 241, accompanies a vocal line.

Ex. 243   Belshazzar's Feast p11   *Walton*

An ostinato from a polytonal passage is given in Example 244. Tonalities of F major and F-sharp major are suggested. The use of ostinato to create polytonal implications provides many interesting possibilities.

Ex. 244   Piano Sonata (1916) p3   *Milhaud*

The final example has two ostinato lines, both in eighth notes but moving independently. Of particular interest is the polytonal implication of the free voice in the work of a composer generally regarded as a conservative. That the A major and E-flat relationship is no mere coincidence is made clear by the subsequent statement of the same material with the tonalities reversed. The tritone has thematic significance in this symphony.

Ex. 245   Symphony No. 4 p42, p62   *Sibelius*

Methods of harmonic motivation cannot be divorced from the harmonies they articulate and the melodies they support. When melodic, harmonic, and rhythmic resources are richly varied as they are in twentieth century music, accompaniment patterns are correspondingly endowed. The motivating devices facilitate composing by providing harmonic backgrounds with rhythmic interest while minimizing the problems of creating new patterns, new chords, and new lines. Since the motivating techniques come rather easily, composers sometimes succumb to the temptation to use them to excess.

Suggested Assignments

1. Find and analyze interesting examples of harmonic motivation in twentieth century music for various mediums.

2. Motivate the block chord progression given in Example 127 or some similar chord pattern in the following ways:

   a. In a pattern of three or four notes like an Alberti bass.
   b. With irregularly spaced accents on repeated chords.
   c. In arpeggio figures with more than an octave compass.
   d. In an asymmetric meter.
   e. With changing time signatures.
   f. Over or under an ostinato.

It is not necessary to include every note of each chord in the motivated versions. Incomplete chords are common in rhythmically animated harmonic progressions.

3. Compose melodies to go with the more effective accompaniments devised for Assignment 2.

4. Write a short harmonic progression as an ostinato accompaniment to a rhythmically independent original melody.

5. Write a two part ostinato which involves imitation.

6. Compose a melody and an ostinato accompaniment which together have polytonal implications.

CHAPTER **XII**

Thematic Metamorphosis

Repetition is basic to the language of music. Meaningful music without repetition is almost inconceivable, and it is usually detectable even in the music of those few composers who strive to avoid it. For most composers it is not a question of eliminating repetition but of sustaining interest, which lags when literal repetition is excessive. Several procedures for modifying repetition which preserve its unifying values without placing interest in jeopardy are at the disposal of composers. The application of these procedures to thematic material produces the metamorphoses so characteristic of the compositional process.

Though exact reiteration has its place in music, modified repetition is more prevalent and useful. Nuances and instrumentation may vary in repetitions which otherwise are literal, but more significant changes involve pitch and rhythm. Such modifications applied to motives and themes sustain interest for extended periods with a minimum of source material. The exhaustive use of a few germ motives is highly conducive to essential unity.

These facts have long been common knowledge, and the imaginative and skillful manipulation of thematic material is a continuing art, not an innovation. The processes of thematic transformation originated in the distant past, but their recent manifestations deserve attention.

Transposition and Sequence

The modification closest to exact repetition but still capable of providing variety is that of octave transposition. Though rhythm, line, and tonality remain the same, the theme is brought into the register of other instruments or shifted to a different register of the same instrument by octave transposition. This type of repetition has the advantage of being immediately apparent to the most casual listener without being utterly lacking in variety. Example 246 shows a melody with interesting contour and internal organization and its octave transposition. A study of these two excerpts in context substantiates the value of octave transposition in modified repetition.

Ex. 246　Daphnis and Chloe p10, p19　　　　　　　　　*Ravel*

Transposition by intervals other than the octave provides additional variety by implying either a different tonal center or a change of harmony, and intervallic relationships may be altered. Example 247 consists of a one measure motive repeated sequentially, each time a third lower. The first and third measures have identical patterns, but the second has a minor third in place of a major third, an augmented fourth in place of one of the perfect fourths, and a diminished fifth in place of a perfect fifth.

Ex. 247　Symphony No. 7 p5　　　　　　　　　*Sibelius*

Interest is added to the sequential treatment of the motive in Example 248 by the slight rhythmic shift in the repetition and the change in relationship between the parts. The two upper voices are repeated sequentially a minor seventh higher with the top part doubled an octave below. The bass also is repeated sequentially, but a perfect fourth lower, providing a fresh relationship. Even those who generally regard sequences as excessively repetitious would find little fault with this imaginative use of the device.

Ex. 248   Divertimento p10   *Piston*

Systematic Modifications of Contour

Every musical line inherently has four basic forms: *original, inversion, retrograde,* and *retrograde inversion.* The inverted form presents the theme upside-down or as if seen in a mirror, going down where the original goes up and up where the original goes down. The retrograde form is like the original played backwards from the end to the beginning. Retrograde inversion is the retrograde form of the inversion or the original upside-down and backwards. All three of these modifications pose certain problems of perception to the listener, but they have persisted in the musical vocabulary for an extended period down to the present time. With but slight alteration all four forms of the theme, original, inversion, retrograde, and retrograde inversion appear in the contemporary fugue from which Example 249 is taken.

Ex. 249   Ludus Tonalis: Fuga Tertia in F   *Hindemith*

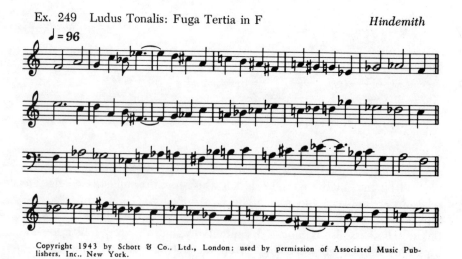

Of the modifications illustrated above, the retrograde forms are more obscure, and hence less useful for purposes of unity. The inverted form, which preserves the rhythmic pattern, is most readily perceived as a derivation of the original. Consequently it is capable of contributing to both unity and variety. The principle of inversion may be applied mechanically, interval by interval, or with some freedom as demonstrated in Example 250. The second version of the theme is essentially, but not exactly, an inversion of the first.

Ex. 250   Mikrokosmos Vol. VI No. 146   *Bartok*

Still greater freedom in the application of the principle of inversion is illustrated in Example 251. The identity of the altered form is conspicuous in spite of the inversion of some intervals and slight changes in rhythm.

Ex. 251   Symphony No. 5 p3, p45   *Shostakovich*

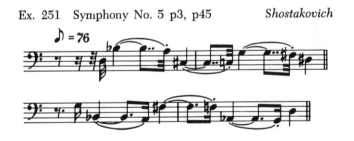

Although inversion is used more extensively, except possibly in the twelve-tone technique, retrograde and retrograde inversions are found in nonrow works. In Number 18 of Schoenberg's *Pierrot Lunaire*, the four top parts from the middle on are an exact retrograde of the first half. The *Postludium* of Hindemith's *Ludus Tonalis* is a literal retrograde inversion of the *Praeludium* with the voices reversed from top to bottom.

It is not feasible to quote these extended works, but they are well worth studying.

Systematic Modifications of Rhythm

Inversion, retrograde, and retrograde inversion are systematic ways of modifying musical lines. Rhythmic patterns also may be altered systematically by increasing or decreasing the value of the notes by a constant ratio, most often double or half. Increasing the rhythmic values is known as *augmentation*, decreasing them as *diminution*.

Example 252 shows two versions of a theme, the second with rhythmic values double those of the first. The slightly faster tempo of the second does not offset entirely the broadening effect of the increased values.

Ex. 252   Symphony No. 5 p109, p146   *Shostakovich*

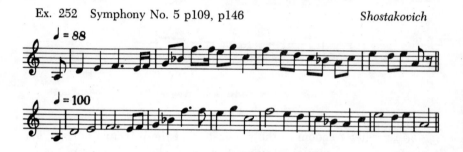

Example 253 also shows two versions of a theme with the second in augmentation. In this case the tempo change is from *Andantino* to *Allegro giusto*. The net result is that the theme proceeds at the same rate both times in spite of the change of tempo. Augmentation and diminution in notation are effective both for changing the speed of a theme and for preserving the same speed through changes of tempo.

Ex. 253   Piano Concerto No. 3 p71, p108   *Prokofieff*

A somewhat different type of rhythmic change is illustrated in Example 254. The material in each measure of the two versions corresponds, but the number of beats in a measure is reduced from three to two. At the same time, the metronome mark is reduced, but not sufficiently to make the two forms move at the same rate. Adjustments are made in the other values, but the three equal notes in a measure are preserved as a triplet.

Ex. 254   Mathis der Maler p42, p77   *Hindemith*

Sometimes only a portion of a theme is used in augmentation or diminution. This is the case in Example 255. The values of the first seven notes in the second version double those of the first, but from there on, though there are some changes in rhythm and line, the material of the measures corresponds.

Ex. 255   Symphony No. 1 p67, p100   *Piston*

Augmentation may be used within the theme, as it is in Example 256. The material of the first measure appears again in the last three measures with increased values. The two forms of this idea enclose two related measures, for an interesting thematic structure.

Ex. 256   Symphony No. 1 p1   *Barber*

Within the space of seven score pages, Shostakovich uses the same thematic motive in augmentation, in diminution, and in various transpositions.

Ex. 257   Symphony No. 1 p74, p78, p80   *Shostakovich*

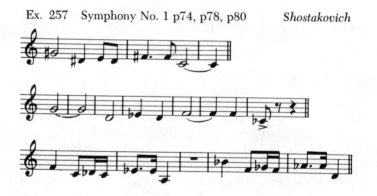

Other Modifications

Besides the systematic methods of modifying themes and motives, there are other means of alteration which are not easily classified, and the systematic principles may be applied freely and in combinations. The thematic material of the passage quoted from *Appalachian Spring* demonstrates some of the possibilities. It consists of nine repetitions with various modifications of a single four note motive. The second statement of the motive has the value of the first two notes reduced. The next version is a partial inversion, and the one immediately following transposes this and extends the last note. The fifth appearance repeats the second; the next preserves the rhythm of these but expands two of the intervals. The seventh is a transposition of the third, the eighth a transposition of the fourth. The final version repeats the previous one, but extends the last note. This type of thematic construction assures a high degree of unity, and used skillfully, adequate interest.

Ex. 258   Appalachian Spring p24   *Copland*

Roy Harris uses a different approach in the following thematic lines from his *Third Symphony*. Organic unity is sensed within each theme and between all three, but there is little actual repetition or obvious manipulation. This type of thematic transformation is conceived and perceived by instinct essentially, and no significant use is made of traditional formulas. As a result the unifying features do not yield readily to systematic analysis, though they are apparent and effective.

Ex. 259   Symphony No. 3 p24, p25, p28   *Harris*

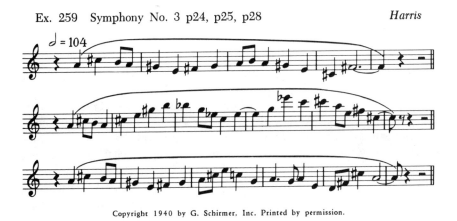

The opening motive of the Bartok *Second String Quartet* is altered continually in subsequent entrances as the movement progresses. The following are just a few of its many guises. Only the rhythm and direction of the first three notes are constant. Other rhythmic values are lengthened and shortened; intervals are expanded and contracted; direction of the line is changed; but the identity of the motive is never in doubt.

Ex. 260   String Quartet No. 2   *Bartok*

More elaborate thematic metamorphosis occurs in Bartok's *Fourth Quartet*. Example 261 shows several versions of a single motive which dominates both the first and last (fifth) movements. The initial statement of the motive is by the cello near the beginning of the first movement. It is taken up almost immediately by the violin in its original form and then inverted (line 1 of the example). The next version shows the motive with the chromatic intervals expanded and the rhythm modified. This, too, is inverted. The other forms are from the fifth movement. In the first of these and its inversion the previous pattern is shifted rhythmically and extended. The intervals and compass are expanded further in the next version. Its essential features are preserved in a free inversion. The final version of the motive shown can scarcely be related to the original motive without reference to the intervening transformations. The motive has become a melodic line the last half of which is a free retrograde of the first half.

Ex. 261   String Quartet No. 4 p4, p8, p45, p46, p47   *Bartok*

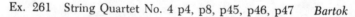

Peruse complete works at random for additional examples of the many and varied methods of thematic transformation. All of them will not be found in any one composition, but some of them will be. Thematic metamorphosis is basic in the construction of extended musical forms, and the ability to recognize thematic elements in all their mutations is prerequisite to intelligent performing and listening.

Suggested Assignments

1. Locate examples of augmentation and diminution in recent music. Determine whether the changes in note values were made to alter the flow of the melodies or to preserve the original movement in a different tempo.

2. Catalog the different versions of the motive in the first measure of Example 256 used in Barber's *First Symphony.*

3. Find examples of thematic metamorphosis in the first and last movements of Bartok's *String Quartet No. 5.*

4. Write a motive and extend it by varied sequential repetition.

5. Compose a theme which is equally effective as nearly as possible in its original, inverted, retrograde, and inverted retrograde forms.

6. Write a theme in which a motive is used in augmentation and/or free inversion.

7. Construct an extended theme from a single concise motive by applying some of the procedures outlined in this chapter. Strive for interesting contour and logical organization.

8. Write three different but similar melodies related in the manner of those in Example 259.

9. Create a brief motive and then write several modifications of it which would be useful in an extended composition. Time permitting, compose a short movement using this motive and its modifications as unifying elements.

CHAPTER XIII

Imitative Procedures

The practice of imitation dates back almost as far as the art of sounding tones together. For centuries strictly observed conventions were formidable barriers to contrapuntal fluency. Writing imitation in conformity to baroque and classic precepts was a notable achievement constituting somewhat of an end in itself. It is hardly necessary to mention that this is no longer the case. The twentieth century permissiveness previously observed in connection with melodic invention and the treatment of dissonance applies equally to melodies in contrapuntal associations. Contrapuntal intricacy is not the evidence of technical mastery and the assurance of quality it once was now that the obstacles which formerly thwarted novices have been removed. H. L. Mencken is supposed to have said that writing free verse was like playing tennis with the net down. The analogy might well be applied to writing dissonant counterpoint.

This is not to say that the artistic and esthetic values of imitation have diminished but only that unrestrained accessibility increases the proclivity for excessive and mechanical usage. Contrapuntal manipulations not motivated by a genuine creative impulse quickly degenerate into a mere display of pedantry. Imaginative contrapuntal writing remains today as always one of the composer's most versatile and valuable modes of expression.

Though counterpoint and imitation are used almost synonymously, much effective contrapuntal music does not involve imitation. Contrapuntal associations of independent lines are difficult to classify and analyze, and it is for this reason alone that the following examples are drawn exclusively from imitative passages. They illustrate adaptations peculiar to the twentieth century of previously accepted practices, all of which persist to the present time. The relationships illustrated are equally possible between nonimitative contrapuntal lines. The one contrapuntal style exclusively a product of this century, the twelve-tone technique, is the subject of the next chapter.

Direct Imitation

In traditional counterpoint dissonances are associated with stepwise motion, but in keeping with other contemporary practices this principle has been discarded. The first example is one of direct imitation at an interval and distance which might be found in any period, an octave above at the distance of one beat. The casual way in which dissonant intervals are left by leap sets it apart from the past. The effect of the dissonances is minimized by their short duration and their unaccented position at the end of beats.

Ex. 262   Symphony No. 5 p3   *Shostakovich*

Example 263 also has octave imitation at the distance of one beat and dissonances left by leap. Beginning the two parts together and making the upper one the follower by extending its first note is a novel touch.

Ex. 263   Belshazzar's Feast p27   *Walton*

Imitative voices may be, and frequently are, accompanied by free parts. Example 264 has a pedal point between two voices in canon at the distance of one measure. The precise imitation of intervals starting

a major third below (compound intervals, such as tenths, are considered
as simple intervals in analyzing imitation) gives the appearance of polytonality, but all the notes are in the harmonic or natural forms of D
minor except the E-flat and D-flat at the end. The imitation is real (exact interval for interval) only for the first four measures. In the fifth
measure the imitation becomes tonal, with a major second in the follower
imitating a minor second in the leader, and in the sixth measure the
imitation ceases. The asymmetric divisions produce an effective inter-
locking of rhythmic motion between the imitating voices.

Ex. 264   Ballad of Heroes p19   *Britten*

A descending line in thirds accompanies a curious bit of imitation
with typical twentieth century features in Example 265. The imitation
starts a half beat later in the measure than the statement, producing a
shift in the rhythmic stresses. The intervals are modified in such a way
that some notes of the statement are imitated at the unison, some a half
step lower, and one a whole step lower.

Ex. 265   Pierrot Lunaire p5   *Schoenberg*

Imitation at intervals other than the fourth and fifth is more characteristic of the present time than of earlier periods. Schoenberg exploits this possibility in Example 266. Against a rich harmonic background, not shown, the two voices exchange thematic fragments. The upper imitates the lower an augmented octave above, and the lower imitates the upper a major seventh below.

Ex. 266   Verklaerte Nacht p14   *Schoenberg*

More recent but more conventional imitation is shown in Example 267. The imitation at the fifth above and the octave below, as well as the suspension-like resolution of some of the dissonances, could have come right out of Bach. The academic approach perhaps is to be expected in a fugue. Only the angularity of the lines and complex harmonic implications betray its twentieth century origin.

Ex. 267   Ludus Tonalis: Fuga Octava   *Hindemith*

Close fragmentary imitation producing pyramid effects is a common contemporary device illustrated in Example 268. The rising fifth in the first voice is imitated by fourths in the succeeding voices. In conventional music this would be tonal imitation, but as used here it does not accomplish the classic function of preserving the tonality. Successive imitations a major sixth, a major third, a major seventh, and an augmented fourth above the original lead to interesting vertical structures.

Ex. 268   Te Deum p44   *Kodaly*

In the four voice imitation of Example 269 the first note of alternate entrances is transposed down an octave to avoid overlapping in the imitation, which otherwise is at the unison. The imitation of the first pair is at the distance of one measure, the second pair at the distance of two measures for added variety. The imitative counterpoint is followed immediately by a thematic fragment in parallel seventh chords, but with no apparent inconsistency of style.

Ex. 269   Piano Concerto No. 3 p59   *Bartok*

Modified Imitation

The methods of thematic modification discussed in Chapter XII are used imitatively, and Hindemith's *Ludus Tonalis* is virtually a catalog

of these procedures. Example 270 begins with a fugue subject in its
original form and in augmentation. Two measures later the augmented
form enters in the soprano. In the seventh measure, while the augmented
form is continuing in the soprano, the inverted form enters in the bass.
The middle voice presents fragments from both the original and inverted
forms of the subject.

Ex. 270   Ludus Tonalis: Fuga Nona   *Hindemith*

Example 271 presents the same subject as Example 270 with the
retrograde form and an incomplete retrograde inversion in imitation one
measure apart.

Ex. 271   Ludus Tonalis: Fuga Nona   *Hindemith*

In the Hindemith examples just cited the imitation occasionally varies slightly from the statement. This is common practice, but imitation also may be exact. This is the case in Example 272, where every interval of the second voice is a precise inversion of the corresponding interval of the first, though some are spelled enharmonically. Both types of imitation, literal and free, are useful.

Ex. 272   Pierrot Lunaire No. 17   *Schoenberg*

Application of the principle of free inversion is illustrated in Example 273. The first, third, and fourth voices are in direct imitation at the octave. The second and fifth entrances two octaves apart invert the contour of the others, but not the precise intervals. The middle line breaks the imitation in the fifth measure, probably for harmonic reasons. Unlike some composers, Bartok is inclined to make compromises in imitation for the sake of sonority.

Ex. 273   Piano Concerto No. 3 p32   *Bartok*

Example 274 has inverted imitation with an interesting rhythmic shift. Halfway through, the imitating voice drops from two to three eighths behind the leader.

Ex. 274   Mikrokosmos Vol. VI No. 141   *Bartok*

In Example 275 the simultaneous free inversion, or mirroring, makes an effective counterpoint to the theme. It lacks the rhythmic interplay of free counterpoint or imitation with a delayed entrance, but it is contrapuntally more interesting than melodic doubling, to which it is related.

Ex. 275   Concerto for Orchestra p68   *Bartok*

Example 276 is an intrinsically simple piece of writing which on closer examination reveals some intricate contrapuntal processes. In the order of entrance, the second voice is an augmentation of the first; the third is an inversion of both, an augmentation of the first and a diminution of the second; the fourth is an inversion of the third and a diminution of the second. The second measure repeats the procedure. The analysis of this passage sounds much more complicated than the music, which is convincing evidence of the contrapuntal mastery of the composer.

Ex. 276   Piano Concerto No. 3 p36   *Bartok*

Contrapuntal skill is not something with finite limits mastered in a course or two. Its development is a continuing process which extends far beyond formal training. The late works of Mozart and Beethoven attest to their growth in this regard throughout productive careers. The magnitude of their genius and that of other composers past and present can be fully appreciated only by those who have tried their hand at it. Cultivation and admiration of contrapuntal skill go hand in hand.

The preceding examples and following assignments show how contrapuntal techniques have been and may be used in contemporary idioms. Knowing how and when to use them are necessary facets of the composer's craft, and sensitivity to his efforts is a prime objective for performers and listeners.

Suggested Assignments

1. From selected or assigned contrapuntal passages in contemporary works, determine:
   a. The intervals of imitation.
   b. The distance of imitation.
   c. The harmonic implications of the combined lines.
   d. The modifications, if any, in the imitating lines.

2. Using Example 262 as a model, write a two part imitative counterpoint with each part doubled at the octave in which dissonances are treated freely. The following procedure facilitates writing imitative counterpoint:

   a. Write the leader for the distance of the imitation.
   b. Copy this where it occurs in the follower with the desired transposition and modifications, if any.
   c. Write a suitable counterpoint to the follower in the leader. Strive for logical contour, flow, and continuity.
   d. Copy the new material of the leader in the follower.
   e. Repeat the process for the duration of the imitation.

3. Write a two part imitative counterpoint at an interval other than an octave accompanied by a free voice, which may be a nonimitative line, a pedal point, or an ostinato.

4. Write an example of two part imitative counterpoint with imitation at a dissonant interval. The imitation may be exact or free.

5. Write a three part canonic passage which has contemporary harmonic implications.

6. Create a pyramid effect by a series of close imitative entrances.

7. Write a brief example of two part counterpoint with inverted imitation.

8. Write a brief example of two part counterpoint with imitation in augmentation.

9. Write a melody which is effective with simultaneous mirroring in the manner of Example 275. Modifications in the mirror are permissible to improve the harmonic effect.

10. Compose a short work in two or three parts for the medium of your choice employing several of the contrapuntal procedures outlined in this chapter.

CHAPTER XIV

The Twelve-
Tone Technique

The *twelve-tone* or *tone row* technique is one of the most significant innovations of the twentieth century. The materials and methods of other contemporary styles, except for the most recent and radical, are largely extensions and modifications of previous practices, but the row technique introduces procedures which are essentially new. Links with the past are not totally lacking, but elements with no direct antecedents predominate. This style was not, however, conceived as a revolt against tradition but rather as a means of organizing and systematizing tendencies already prevalent in music. These tendencies created certain problems for which the twelve-tone technique was proposed as a solution. Its formulation as a method of composition more than any other concept of comparable scope was the work of a single artistic mind, that of Arnold Schoenberg. This achievement alone would merit his position as one of the creative geniuses of our age.

The eventual position of the row technique in music remains to be seen. The perspective of roughly half a century is inadequate for a final judgment, but its impact on twentieth century music is enormous and mounting. Many contemporaries employ this method of composition exclusively, and none are free of its influence. For this reason knowledge of the methods and objectives of row composing is valuable not only in comprehending the music resulting directly from this system, but of contemporary music in general. This chapter aims to foster understanding by developing a working knowledge of the method. Those interested in pursuing the study further will find available several books and articles which deal exclusively and exhaustively with the subject.°

°See Suggested Assignment 1 at the end of this chapter.

To understand the twelve-tone technique one must first understand the situation which engendered it. Early in the century musical materials were expanded to the point where the foundations of conventional tonal organization (tonality, scales, and root progressions) were being shaken. Several of the contributing factors have been examined in previous chapters.

Some composers were content to extend the resources within recognizable limits which preserved essential structural functions. The concept of tonality could be broadened without being lost. Extensive chromaticism and the substitution of modal and synthetic scales for major and minor would not necessarily dissipate the values of selective scales. Increasingly complex sonorities could be introduced, and chord roots could move freely without becoming unintelligible. Within these boundaries traditional methods of organizing tonal materials were adequate.

Other composers were inclined to traverse these boundaries in the pursuit of tonal relationships without tonality, not based on selective scales, using tonal aggregates indescribable in conventional terms, and dissonance almost to the exclusion of consonance. Under these circumstances conventional methods of tonal organization cease to function. To replace them Schoenberg devised a procedure he called *A Method of Composing with Twelve Tones which Are Related only with One Another*. This is the system commonly referred to as the *twelve-tone, note series,* or *tone row* technique.

Formation of the Series

Essentially, the system consists of setting up a sequence of the twelve notes of the chromatic scale and repeating them in a fixed order constantly and exclusively throughout a composition. Twelve different notes are used, and none is repeated. The crux of the series lies in the order of tones and the intervals between them. The twelve tones in their fixed order are known collectively as the *series, row, set,* or *Grundgestalt.* Isolated, the series usually is represented in notes of equal value with a limited compass. The first version is designated as the *original form* or *basic set* to distinguish it from subsequent modifications.

There are no definite rules regarding the construction of the series, but a few principles beyond the requirements of using all twelve tones with no repetitions generally are observed. Music in the row technique is by nature atonal, and suggestions of tonality in the series are foreign to the style. Adherence to the order of the series assures equal use of all tones and minimizes the possibility of any note, because of emphasis, asserting itself as a tonic.

Variety in interval relationships is desirable. Examples 277 and 278 are typical, each with five different intervals. These intervals and their inversions, available through octave transposition of one of the tones, comprise eight of the eleven possible. In Example 277 the tritone, the minor third, and its inversion are missing. In Example 278 the tritone, the major second, and its inversion are missing.

Ex. 277   String Quartet No. 4   *Schoenberg*

Ex. 278   12 Short Piano Pieces   *Krenek*

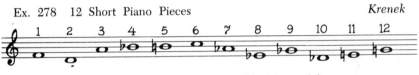

The possibilities for series formations are almost infinite. For maximum variety, all eleven intervals can be incorporated in the series, though half will be inversions of the other half. More often, for added unity, characteristic interval relationships are repeated, as in Example 277. In this series, notes 8-9-10 are a retrograde inversion of notes 1-2-3 transposed. Notes 10-11-12 are a transposed mirror of notes 3-4-5.

Example 279 also has repetitions of characteristic interval relationships. The series is shown as it occurs in the solo violin part. It has only thirds and major seconds, one spelled enharmonically as a diminished third. Enharmonic spellings are used freely since equally tempered tuning is taken for granted. Of the first nine notes in the example, any consecutive three form a triad. Each type—major, minor, augmented, and diminished—is represented, and all but the diminished is repeated.

Ex. 279   Violin Concerto p4   *Berg*

Twelve-tone Lines

Theoretically, themes with all twelve tones and no repetitions should be conceived spontaneously, but this would be very unlikely for anyone not thoroughly conditioned in the system. Invariably with students, the row is worked out first and the characteristic shape and rhythm of the theme is derived later. The row itself is not a theme, though it is the source of all thematic material. Before becoming a theme, it must have a distinctive rhythm and contour. In evolving a theme from the series, certain liberties are customary. Notes may be used in any octave and repeated freely as long as their position in the order is not disturbed. Example 280 is based on the series of Example 277.

Ex. 280   String Quartet No. 4 p1   *Schoenberg*

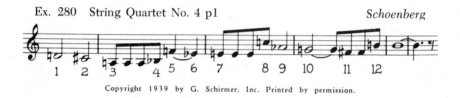

Copyright 1939 by G. Schirmer, Inc. Printed by permission.

The series may be transposed to any degree of the chromatic scale. Example 281 is based on the same series as Example 280 transposed a diminished fifth. The rhythm is identical, but different octave transpositions are used.

Ex. 281   String Quartet No. 4 p18   *Schoenberg*

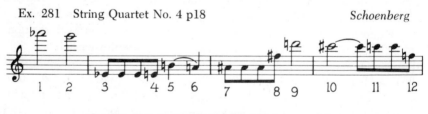

Copyright 1939 by G. Schirmer, Inc. Printed by permission.

Example 282 is a different theme derived from still another transposition of the same series. It also illustrates an additional type of permissible repetition, that of a small fragment. G-flat and F, notes 9 and 10 of the series in this transposition, are repeated before notes 11 and 12 appear. This procedure is common. Repetitions of small figures and patterns which can be perceived as such are used freely in the same manner as repeated notes. This also applies in trills, tremolo, accompanying and embellishing figures.

Ex. 282   String Quartet No. 4 p63   *Schoenberg*

In addition to transposition, all the methods of systematically modifying the contour of themes and motives are applied also to the series
The use of it in the original form and in inversion, retrograde, and retrograde inversion is part of the fundamental concept of the method. With
the twelve transpositions of each of these four basic shapes, forty-eight
versions exist for each series.

Example 283 comes from a transposition and interval inversion of
the row given in Example 277 and used in Examples 280-282. Using the
same rhythmic pattern as Examples 280 and 281, Example 283 illustrates the principle of *isorhythm,* that is, repeating a rhythmic pattern
with a different contour. Isorhythm is common in twelve-tone compositions.

Ex. 283   String Quartet No. 4 p10   *Schoenberg*

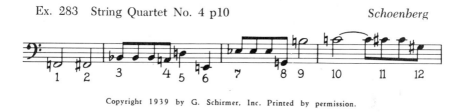

The retrograde form of the same row is the basis for Example 284.
It has rhythmic features of the previous examples, but does not repeat
the entire pattern.

Ex. 284   String Quartet No. 4 p1   *Schoenberg*

Example 285 is a rhythmically independent theme derived from the retrograde inversion of the Example 277 series.

Ex. 285   String Quartet No. 4 p30   *Schoenberg*

Twelve-tone melodies are found occasionally in the works of composers who do not use the technique customarily. Example 286 is from an isolated instance where Bloch employed the system. The line, in spite of its twelve tones, is not without tonal implications.

Ex. 286   Sinfonia Breve p27   *Bloch*

Bartok does not use the twelve-tone method in his *Violin Concerto,* but it has a theme with all the notes and no repetitions.

Ex. 287   Violin Concerto p12   *Bartok*

Twelve-tone Texture

The foregoing examples demonstrate the application of the twelve-tone method to the formation of single lines. In strict twelve-tone composition, not just the thematic material, but the entire texture is derived from the series. Twelve-tone composition is primarily a contrapuntal procedure, and as such, attention is focused on the construction and combination of lines. Very free vertical associations compensate somewhat for the strict adherence to the order of the series in all parts. Sonority, as a phenomenon independent of linear combinations, is of so little importance in the style, principles of harmonic structure and progression are not given by its theorists, nor are harmonic formulas detectable in the compositions.

Harmonies, in the sense of vertical sounds, consist of any combination of any number of notes. The choice is largely determined by the order of the series, though considerable flexibility is possible in spacing. Clusters and congestions generally are avoided. Sharp dissonances usually are spaced in a manner which emphasizes their resonance and minimizes their harshness, except for special effects. Octave doubling and unisons, with few exceptions, are not used in the style. Conventional consonant chords occur but rarely and are permitted only when they have little connotation of tonality. The vertical sounds stem from the series, but the series can be manipulated to produce almost any desired sonority. Some series are constructed with a view to the harmonic effect of certain groups of consecutive notes.

Though sonority is a secondary consideration, it is not ignored by composers in the style. Climactic points in the form and in the lines are associated with increased tension in the vertical structure. Harmonic tension is related to dissonance, but the two cannot be considered synonymous. Other factors, such as spacing, scoring, dynamics, rhythm, and tempo, also influence tension.

The degree of dissonance can be reckoned roughly by the number and kind of dissonant intervals comprised between all component parts. Seconds and sevenths are dissonant. Minor seconds and major sevenths are more dissonant than major seconds and minor sevenths. Perfect fourths are consonant or dissonant depending upon the context. In combination with other intervals their effect usually is that of a consonance. Tritones are dissonant, but in atonal music they do not demand the prescribed resolution associated with them in tonal music. The other intervals are consonant.

In music of more than one part, there are several ways of deriving the material of the various parts from the basic series. The notes of one form of the series may be distributed between all the parts. Or, each part may have its own form of the series, in which case two or more forms of the series will progress concurrently. When more than one form of the series is in progress, the notes of the various forms may be exchanged between the different voices. It is not a requirement to complete a series in the same part. Notes from a series may be used simultaneously to make chords. The vertical arrangement of chords so formed is not determined by the order of the series. Chord tones may be distributed in any order from top to bottom without violating the required sequence.

These generalizations are oversimplified, and exceptions are to be found. They are, however, adequately valid to serve as a guide for initiates in the style. The following analysis of excerpts from a mature work, the *Concerto for Violin op. 36*, by the originator of the method of composing with twelve tones provides added insight to its functions.

Example 288 gives the forms of the series used in Examples 289-291. The first line gives the basic set or original form (0). The next three lines are the inversion (I), retrograde (R), and retrograde inversion (RI) respectively at the pitch of their initial appearance in the concerto. The last two lines give the original and inverted forms of the series transposed to the pitches used in the second movement (OT and IT). In the analysis of Examples 289-291, the notes of all forms of the series are numbered consecutively from 1 to 12, unlike the previous examples in which the retrograde forms were numbered in reverse order.

Ex. 288   Violin Concerto   *Schoenberg*

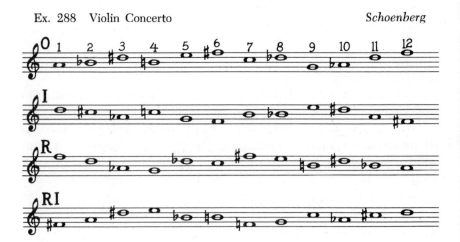

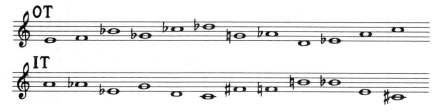

The complete series is stated in its original form in the upbeat and the first three measures of Example 289, distributed between the solo and the accompaniment. The minor seconds between 1-2 and 7-8 are set sequentially with the same rhythm. The other notes of the series used in pairs provide the accompaniment. The intervals between 9-10 and 11-12 are repeated alternately in a fashion characteristic of this passage.

The inverted form of the series starting on D is the basis of measures 4-7. This series is constructed in such a way that the inversion of the first six notes starting on D does not duplicate any of the first six notes of the original starting on A. Consequently, there is no duplication between the last six notes of these two forms of the series, either. The violin uses the same notes from this form of the series as from the previous one with a similar rhythm producing a free mirror of the line.

In measures 8-11 the full series in its original form appears in the solo part. This appearance establishes the order of the tones, since it is not possible in the prior statements to determine which of two notes sounding together comes first. This original form in the violin is accompanied by the inverted form.

Starting in measure 11 the solo and accompaniment exchange forms of the series. Using the first six notes of the inversion, the violin repeats the rhythm used with the previous original form. This inversion in the solo is accompanied by the material of measures 1-4, rhythmically compressed and with some additional repetitions of intervals. The solo line of the opening is now in the bass.

The retrograde form of the series first appears starting in measure 15. Distributed between the parts, it is completed in measure 16. The retrograde inversion follows immediately, also distributed between the parts.

The original form reappears in measure 20. In this statement the first six notes in the melody are accompanied by two three-note chords using the remaining six notes. The same procedure is repeated starting in measure 21 using the inversion of the series.

Ex. 289   Violin Concerto p3   *Schoenberg*

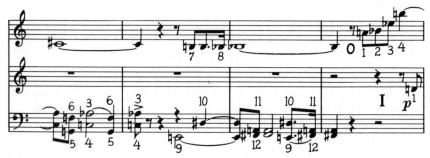

Ex. 289   page 2

Example 290 is from the beginning of the second movement of the Schoenberg *Violin Concerto*. It uses the original and inverted forms of the same series, both transposed down a perfect fourth. This parallels the tonal practice of having second movements in a related key.

The series is treated somewhat more freely in this example, perhaps on the assumption that it is more familiar by this time. The statement of the original form occupies the solo for twelve measures. The first six notes of the original are accompanied by the first six notes of the inversion, but the accompaniment goes through the first half of its series four times. Likewise, tones 7-12 of the original are accompanied by tones 7-12 of the inversion, with those of the inversion repeated five times.

Ex. 290   Violin Concerto p29   *Schoenberg*

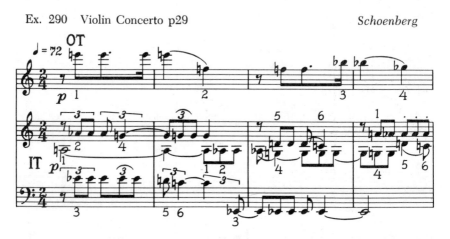

Example 291 is the beginning of the *Finale* of the same work, using the inverted and original forms of the series untransposed. This also parallels conventional key relationship in tonal music. The procedure is very similar to that in the second movement. In this case five repetitions of the first half and four repetitions of the second half of the original

Ex. 291 Violin Concerto p45 *Schoenberg*

accompany a single extended statement of the inversion in the solo. The four-note chords in the accompaniment are good examples of the vertical arrangement of the series tones.

Anton Webern, who was a student of Schoenberg, applied the principles of serial composition in a very personal way. His style matured slowly over a period of years. It is characterized by extremely sparse texture and highly concentrated motivic structure. His works, which invariably are of short duration, create the impression of having been distilled to the point where only the barest essentials remain. He found the intimate mediums of musical expression most congenial and wrote extensively for voice accompanied by piano or a small group of instruments and for uniquely constituted chamber ensembles.

Example 292 is representative of Webern's mature style. The score showing the full instrumentation of his *Symphony Op. 21* is necessary to convey an impresssion of the writing and scoring, which are inseparable in Webern. The discontinuity with more rests than notes, the angularity of the lines with wide leaps spanning dissonant intervals, the pointillistic scattering of notes over the page, and the subdued dynamics are all typical. Full tuttis and fortissimos are hardly to be found in his scores. The technical procedures in Example 292 are also typical. Written strictly in the twelve-tone system, it shows the beginning of a four part canon in contrary motion. The distribution of the canonic lines between different instruments and registers provides additional insight to the style.

It is too soon to pronounce definitive rules for composing with twelve tones, and there are not yet enough works applying the principles in the same way to prescribe universally acceptable common practices. Webern utilized Schoenberg's principles in a manner which produced significantly different results. Many of the younger composers—Karlheinz Stockhausen, Pierre Boulez, and Luigi Nono among them—appear to be directly influenced by Webern and only indirectly by Schoenberg. A new generation of twelve-tone composers is actively engaged in extending the system, especially in the direction of bringing other elements in addition to pitch under serial control, when it is not inventing more revolutionary means to supplant it.

After becoming familiar with the twelve-tone system and music written in it, each musician must make a subjective judgment of its merit just as each composer must decide what to apply, what to modify, and what to discard. Whether one decides to embrace or denounce the system, he will have good company. It has been praised as the only valid twentieth century idiom and condemned as an artistic blind alley already explored to the limits of its potential. Whatever the ultimate de-

Ex. 292 Symphony Op. 21 p1 *Webern*

cision, every musician owes it to himself to know something about the method and to formulate his attitude only after acquiring an intimate knowledge of some music produced by it. A style originated by Schoenberg, adopted by Berg and Webern, and more recently practiced by such venerable composers as Stravinsky, Copland, and Sessions cannot be ignored.

Even those who reject the system for artistic expression find something of value in it as exercise material and as a way of acquiring skill in handling tonal relations uninhibited by tonality. It has been suggested that some day studies in the twelve-tone method may supplant studies in conventional harmony and counterpoint. It may become a discipline used to develop a keen instinct for atonal music, functioning as traditional studies in music theory do now for tonal music. Before this happens, atonality will have to be assimilated as tonality has been in ages past. This is still in the future. The time may never come, or it may be nearer than we think. At this point, who is to say?

Suggested Assignments

1. Read sections of particular interest selected from the following:

    Krenek, Ernst. *Studies in Counterpoint* (G. Schirmer, Inc., New York, 1940).

    Leibowitz, Rene. *Schoenberg and His School* (Philosophical Library, New York, 1949).

    Perle, George. *Serial Composition and Atonality* (University of California Press, Berkeley and Los Angeles, 1962).

    Rufer, Josef. *Composition with Twelve Notes Related to One Another* (Rockliff, London, 1954).

2. Listen to the recording *Twelve-tone Composition* (narration and musical examples), Folkways Records FT3612.

3. Analyze in the manner of Examples 288-291 selected passages from works written in the twelve-tone system. The series usually is more readily traced in the compositions of Schoenberg than in those of his disciples.

4. Write some sample series using all twelve notes of the scale with no repetitions. Contour is of no importance, since octave transpositions will take care of this in the themes, but strive for interesting interval relationships. Experiment with symmetrical rows, that is, rows with patterns repeated in segments or in modified forms of the row, such as the inversion or retrograde.

5. Invent a series like the one in the Schoenberg *Violin Concerto* in which the inversion a fourth lower of the first six tones brings out the remaining six tones.

6. Select one of your series, and write several themes using it in the manner of Examples 280-285.

7. Using the same series, write an extended melody going through the series more than once. Strive for rhythmic interest, unity, and a good contour with logical climax points and cadences.

8. Using only the original form of the series, write a two part exercise, distributing the notes of the series between the two parts.

9. Write out the inversion, retrograde, and retrograde inversion of the same series and at least one transposition of each form.

10. Using any two forms of the series, write a two part counterpoint.

11. Observing the order of the series but using a form or forms of your choice, write an exercise which has vertical sonorities of three or more notes derived from the series.

12. Write a short composition employing the twelve-tone technique in any way you consider to be appropriate. Make an analysis as you compose.

CHAPTER XV

Experiments and Innovations

Previous chapters have explored techniques of twentieth century composition already assimilated into the musical language of our time. Practices and resources which have not yet achieved this status but which are known and used on a limited scale are considered now. Practical and esthetic barriers impede their dissemination, but some of them may merge with the main stream of music in the future. Though the types of music discussed in this chapter are available on recordings, they are seldom performed in concerts. The enthusiasm of composers may be and perhaps should be tempered by this, but their natural curiosity about radical innovations of the day should not be stifled. Critics, listeners, and performers, who sometimes are inclined to resent the unfamiliar and resist inevitable changes, are reminded of the many subsequently recognized masterpieces which were decried as experimental failures at their premieres.

Microtones

Microtones, ie., intervals smaller than semitones, occur in the music of several primitive and oriental cultures, and since the time of the ancient Greeks they have interested composers and theorists of the western world. Those of our century are no exception. Many regard microtones as the next logical step in the development of our musical system. Composers and theorists of this persuasion are motivated by different reasons and propose diverse solutions to the problems of microtonal music.

Microtonal embellishments have been used incidentally in works otherwise restricted to conventional pitches. Bartok's *Violin Concerto* is one of these. Quarter-tone inflections above and below standard pitch are indicated by arrows. The C-sharp in Example 293 with the arrow pointing up is midway between a normal C-sharp and D. The E-flat with the arrow pointing down is midway between a normal E-flat and D. Quarter-tone signs apply within the measure like sharps and flats. They are cancelled by a sharp or flat sign without an arrow or by a natural.

Ex. 293   Violin Concerto p45   *Bartok*

Ernest Bloch uses microtones similarly in his *Quintet for Piano and Strings,* but the notation is different. Diagonal lines positioned before the notes like sharps and flats are used instead of arrows. A line slanting up raises the pitch a quarter tone, and a line slanting down lowers the pitch a quarter tone. A diagonal line appears before each note thus inflected, not just the first of each measure, so no sign is required to cancel the quarter-tone symbols. Only raised quarter tones occur in Example 294, but lowered quarter tones appear elsewhere in the work.

Ex. 294   Quintet p2   *Bloch*

The makeshift notation used for sporadic microtones is inadequate for music which is consistently microtonal. The five line staff designed for seven notes and already taxed by twelve is not readily adaptable to the notation of microtones. However, adaptations of conventional notation have been used for quarter-tone music by several composers. The additional pitches are indicated by supplementary symbols placed before notes like sharps and flats. Quarter-tone signs vary in detail from composer to composer and sometimes even from work to work. Most are modified forms of the basic sharp and flat signs. Modifications include adding appendages to the standard symbols, leaving open and reversing the body of flat signs, and varying from one to three the number of vertical strokes in sharp signs. Notation of this sort has been used by Alois Haba, Ivan Wychnegradsky, Jörg Mager, John Foulds, Willi Moellendorff, R. H. Stein, and Hans Barth. That of Haba shown in Example 295 is typical.

Ex. 295   Quarter-tone Scale   *Haba Notation*

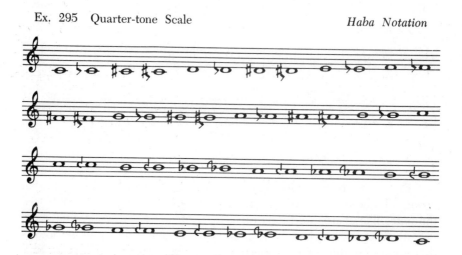

The inability of composers writing quarter-tone music to agree on a common system of notation limits the accessibility of their music. Performers are understandably reluctant to master a complicated system of notation peculiar to a single work or composer. The adoption of standardized notion is prerequisite to more significant achievements in quarter-tone music. Whether the system should follow the lead of Haba and others who continue to use the five line staff or be a new system designed specifically for quarter tones is as yet undecided.

Also undecided is the optimum size for microtones. Scales of 24 quarter tones are only one possibility. Ferruccio Busoni advocated a 36-tone scale with sixths of a tone as the smallest interval. Haba developed a system for notating intervals as small as twelfths of a tone, 72 to an octave, but at latest word he had not utilized intervals this small in compositions. Haba notated his 72-tone scale on a conventional staff with signs used in the manner of sharps and flats, but a totally new approach would seem to be more promising for notating microtones this small.

Julian Carrillo devised one such system which combines precision and flexibility. The note C is represented by the figure 0 (zero). Equal intervals above C are numbered consecutively up to the total within an octave. A chromatic (12-tone) scale would be notated with the numbers

0 through 11. A quarter-tone (24-tone) scale would use the numbers 0 through 23. Busoni's 36-tone scale would require the numbers 0 through 35, and the 96-tone scale used by Carrillo in his *Preludio a Cristobal Colón* employs the numbers 0 through 95. Numbers representing pitches in the octave above middle C are placd on a single line. Numbers above and below the line denote pitches in the next higher and lower octaves, respectively. Still higher and lower octaves are shown by numbers on, above, and below lines that appear and function like ledger lines.

Example 296 shows the pitches of a two-octave G major scale notated in two ways using Carrillo's system. The scale is written using numbers appropriate for conventional semitones, 12 to an octave. Then the same pitches are represented by the numbers used for Carrillo's 96-tone scale. Consecutive numbers in this notation would indicate intervals equal to one-sixteenth of a tone.

Ex. 296   Two-Octave G Major Scale   *Carrillo Notation*

			0	2	4	6	7	9	11	0	2	4	6	7	
7	9	11													

G   A   B   C   D   E   F♯ G   A   B   C   D   E   F♯ G

			0	16	32	48	56	72	88	0	16	32	48	56	
56	72	88													

Rhythmic relationships in Carrillo's notation are shown by stems, flags, and beams attached to the numbers.

The microtones mentioned thus far have been derived from octaves or equally tempered whole tones fractionally divided into equal intervals. Joseph Yasser describes a different way of arriving at a scale with more than twelve tones to an octave. In his book *A Theory of Evolving Tonality*[*], he rejects the arbitrary and mechanical splitting of equal tones into smaller units and advocates extending scale resources by the evolutionary processes he perceives in the music of the past.

He traces the evolution of scales from the pentatonic scale to the 7-tone scale and from the 7-tone scale to the 12-tone scale. The next step in this evolutionary process, according to Yasser, is a 19-tone scale. Of the nineteen tones, the twelve now in general use would be "regular" scale degrees corresponding to seven diatonic notes, and the seven new tones would be "auxiliary" scale degrees, corresponding to the five chromatic notes.

---

[*]New York: American Library of Musicology, 1932.

Mean-tone fifths, slightly smaller than acoustically perfect fifths, provide the basis for a 31-tone scale. Thirty-one mean-tone fifths superimposed form a virtual cycle, and by minute expansion a perfect cycle just as twelve equally tempered fifths do. That is, the thirty-second tone in the one series and the thirteenth in the other duplicate the starting note 18 and 7 octaves higher, respectively. Mean-tone fifths were the basis of an early tuning system, yielding acoustically perfect major thirds, so there is historical precedent for this modification of the fifth. Proponents of the system point not only to the expanded resources of the 31-tone scale but to the improved tuning of conventional intervals as well.

Harry Partch's book, *Genesis of a Music**, examines tuning systems and scale constructions in detail and presents evidence of the superiority of a 43-tone scale of unequal intervals based on ratios. He has constructed instruments, developed notation appropriate to the tonal materials and the instruments (not the same for all of them), trained performers, and produced a quantity of music utilizing the resources of this 43-tone scale.

Partch's activities dramatize the problems confronting composers and performers delving into the realm of microtonal music. Not only are new systems of notation required but new instruments and uniquely trained performers. While it is true that voices, string instruments, and trombones are capable of producing microtonal intervals, their accuracy is limited by the human element. Teachers in these areas are certain to be horrified by the prospect of teaching microtonal intervals. The instruments which have keys, valves, and frets to regulate pitch require radical modifications to depart from or add to present tuning standards.

Pending the perfection of quarter-tone instruments, two pianos tuned a quarter tone apart provide a practical performing medium for quarter-tone music. Conventional pianos, notation, and performing techniques can be used, but only half of the tones are available on each piano. The composer must distribute the notes between the parts accordingly. To play a quarter-tone scale the two players sound notes alternately. The same concept has been embodied in single instruments with two keyboards and two sets of strings tuned a quarter tone apart. Wychnegradsky has composed extensively for an ensemble of four pianos, which he regards as the most suitable medium for quarter-tone music. Two of the pianos are tuned to standard pitch, and the other two are tuned a quarter tone higher.

Ervin M. Wilson has patented the 31-tone keyboard shown in Example 297 for use in conjunction with the 31-tone scale mentioned previously. The interval between digitals with successive numbers is 1/31

---

*Madison: The University of Wisconsin Press, 1949.

of an octave. Traditional notation signs are added to letter names in capitals, but in this application double flats and sharps are not enharmonic equivalents of natural notes. Exotic notation signs for the same pitches are added to lower-case letters. The fractional flat signs are provided by Giuseppe Tartini and the fractional sharp signs by A. D. Fokker.

Ex. 297   Thirty-one Tone Keyboard   *Ervin M. Wilson*

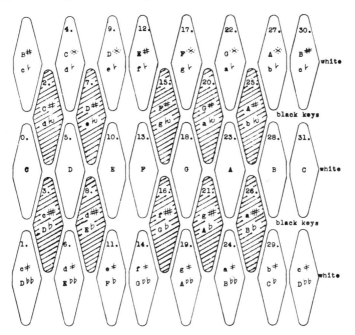

Patent No. 3,012,460 Printed by permission.

The aesthetic value of intervals smaller than a semitone has been studied but not determined. The fact that infinitesimal differences in pitch can be perceived under optimum conditions does not automatically assure their usefulness for artistic purposes. It is unlikely that the smallest perceptible differences in pitch are musically significant, but whether the semitone or some smaller interval represents the ultimate tonal unit is still an open question.

Previously stated problems notwithstanding, the lack of thoroughly compatible systems for notating and performing microtonal and conventional intervals is the most formidable barrier to microtones. Widespread adoption of an incompatible microtonal system would isolate us from our musical heritage and the masterpieces of the past. This, probably

more than anything else, gives reason to ponder before yielding to the
fascination of microtones.

In spite of the difficulties or perhaps because of them, gifted musicians are hard at work solving the problems of microtonal music. Occasional performances and rare record releases attest to their achievements.
Musicians who prevail against the years of conditioning to hear any interval smaller than a semitone as out of tune find the best microtonal
music genuinely alluring. However, it is still in the pioneering stage, and
those attracted to it at this point are more occupied with blazing the
trail than in reaping the harvest.

Rhythmic Reading and Sprechstimme

Rhythmic reading and *sprechstimme,* literally, speaking voice, com-
bine elements of speaking and singing. These vocal styles made notable
debuts in two early twentieth century masterpieces.

In his *Histoire du Soldat* (Soldier's Tale), Stravinsky wrote a voice
part showing only the rhythms. The notation consists of note stems extending down from the middle of the third space of a clefless five line
staff. Without note heads, rhythmic values longer than a quarter note
cannot be written, but they are not required. There are no sustained
tones, and rests complete measures which are not filled by the shorter
values. When the voice has nothing for a full measure or more, the part
is omitted from the score. The notation of the voice part suggests the
speaking quality and normal speech inflections customary in performances. The striking originality of this work is not fully apparent in the
concert and recorded versions which include only the instrumental sections of it.

Ex. 298   Histoire du Soldat p1   *Stravinsky*

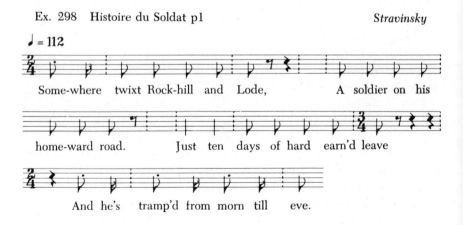

Schoenberg's *Pierrot Lunaire* requires a vocal style known by its German names, *sprechstimme* and *sprechgesang*. *Sprechstimme* is more akin to singing than is rhythmic reading. Pitches and rhythms are both notated. Small crosses on the note stems (above or below whole notes) signify *sprechstimme*, the usual vocal style of the work, which Schoenberg describes in a foreword. The rhythms are to be executed with no more or less freedom than in ordinary singing. The voice is to fall or rise from the notated pitch of each note, in contrast to the sustained pitch of normal singing.

Ex. 299   Pierrot Lunaire No. 7   *Schoenberg*

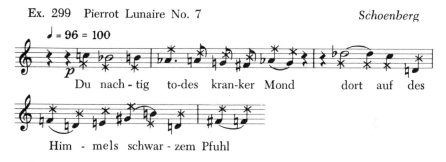

Electronic Music

Electronic devices are a comparatively new source of sound, but already their capabilities have been applied to the production and reproduction of music in a variety of ways. All of the recording, transmitting, receiving, amplifying, and reproducing paraphernalia used in radio, television, and with disc and tape recordings is electronic. The expression *electronic music,* however, is reserved for music which is produced or modified electronically.

Electronic organs are the most familiar of the electronic instruments. Designed to substitute for conventional instruments, they opened no new avenues for composers.

The first electronic instruments to produce basically new sounds and to stimulate the composition of distinctive music were the *Theremin,* the *Trautonium,* and the *Ondes Martenot.* All three of these instruments, which stirred music circles during the 1920s and 1930s, produce an electronic tone controlled by various manual manipulations. These instruments brought music to the threshold of the electronic age, and it arrived with the perfection of tape recording.

Electronic music exists typically in a recorded form. Notation is superfluous, and there are no performers in the usual sense. The "composer" conceives, creates, and executes his electronic compositions. The "live" part of a performance consists of flipping a switch or two and perhaps adjusting the controls. Electronic music is as accessible to an individual in a living room or a group of students in a classroom as to an audience in a concert hall. There are as yet no compelling reasons for people to assemble in groups to hear electronic music. Under these conditions the social functions of music are significantly diminished. As an antidote some composers produce multitrack tape music which for ideal performance requires specially constructed circular concert halls with speakers strategically placed around the perimeter. Motivation for concert attendance is generated by these devices, but they do not entirely compensate for the missing visual stimulus and the absence of empathic communication between performer and listener. Another satisfaction denied electronic music audiences is mutual participation in spontaneous ovations. Lacking established customs in the matter of applause, there is always a moment of embarrassing silence when the immobile loudspeakers from which electronic music has been emanating suddenly become mute as well.

Tracing the sound from the listener back to its source leads from the speakers through the amplifiers and to a disc or tape player. Commercial versions are more apt to be on discs, but disc recordings even of traditional music are copied from master tapes.

. The master tape of an electronic composition *is* the composition. It is a finely edited composite of hundreds or thousands of individually produced segments which may have been recorded directly on sound tape or coded or perforated tapes which were then translated into sounds and recorded. The versatility of tape allows composers unlimited freedom in assembling sounds. Sound impressions recorded on tape are not destroyed when the tape is cut in pieces. Lengths of any size can be spliced together at will, even reversed end for end, and each bit still preserves its original sound impression. The sounds of any number of tapes can be superimposed on a single tape. In mixing the sounds of various tapes, the relative dynamic levels are completely under the control of the composer, and the initial sound recorded on the tape can be modified in a variety of ways. The speed of the tape passing over the playing head can be increased or decreased, raising or lowering the pitch proportionately. Reverberation and echo effects can be added. The timbre can be modified, and various elements can be filtered out. The effects available are limited only by the electronic composer's ingenuity and integrity. The temptation is ever present in the midst of such bountiful resources to indulge in any orgy of sound. The more thoughtful practitioners of the art subject their materials to rigorous controls. The influences of the twelve-tone system and Webern are often acknowledged. Total organization of all the materials and strict compliance with predetermined conditions are possible, and this is one of the attractions exerted by the medium on composers of post-Webernian orientation.

The tape provides the means for capturing and manipulating sounds, but it is not itself a source of sound. The prime sound sources vary in the different electronic music centers. Vladimir Ussachevsky and Otto Luening of Columbia University have included sounds of conventional instruments modified beyond normal recognition in their tape works. They collaborated on *A Poem in Cycles and Bells* for tape recorder and orchestra which uses a tape recorder as a kind of solo instrument with orchestral accompaniment. Their early works utilized some electronically produced sounds, and the installation of the RCA Mark II Electronic Music Synthesizer at the Columbia-Princeton Electronic Music Center makes available to them, to Milton Babbitt, Roger Sessions, and others associated with the center an unparalleled source of electronically produced sound.

A group of composers in Paris using Radiodiffusion Francaise facilities under the direction of Pierre Scheaffer produced a type of tape music known as *musique concrete*. It is characterized by the application of manifold modification procedures to commonplace nonmusical sounds, noises prominent among them.

At the electronic music studio of the Cologne Radio directed by Karlheinz Stockhausen and at the research studio of Siemens in Munich headed by Alexander Schaaf pure or *sinusoidal* tones electronically produced are used as primary sound material. These pure tones differ from conventional tones in that they have no overtones, and hence no color or quality. Sinusoidal tones are combined and electronically modified to produce various tonal qualities. *White noise,* also called *blank noise,* which blankets the full range of frequencies and pitches is also used as an ingredient of German electronic music. Bands of sound filtered from white noise are *colored noise.* Herbert Eimert, Pierre Boulez, Henri Pousseur, Josef Anton Riedl, and Ernst Krenek are among those who have worked in the German studios. Some of their works have included voices and other sounds of nonelectric origin, but as a group their break with the sounds of instruments and nature has been most complete.

Luciano Berio directs a laboratory of the RAI Studio in Milan devoted to electronic music. The Italians apparently have abandoned earlier practices primarily concerned with the amplification of various kinds of noise and now are influenced by both the German and French practices.

Electronic music by nature is microtonal. Microtonal inflections of conventional pitches are available through variations in tape speed. Electronic tone generators are capable of producing every frequency in the audible range and an almost infinite number of pitches. Some electronic music, such as Stockhausen's *Elektronische Studien II**, derive their pitches from a predetermined microtonal scale. Others range freely over the full gamut of the tape recorder's compass.

Having traced the sound from the listener back to its source, the next step presumably would lead to the notation, but not so in electronic music. The actual creation takes place on the tape. A diagram, a plan, or a system may precede the composing on tape, but there is no score of the work in any ordinary sense. This causes a curious dilemma. Recordings cannot be copyrighted. To secure copyright protection for his creative efforts, a tape composer must reduce his recording to some written form even though it cannot be entirely accurate and is superfluous to the realization of the work. There is no standardized system for this. A method which can be at least partially comprehended by the uninitiated is shown in Example 300. The three symbols on the left represent three types of sound. The top is the sine-wave pattern of a pure sinusoidal tone. The middle one is a square-wave pattern created by combining a fundamental sine-wave frequency with an infinite number of electronically generated

Ex. 300   Electronic Music Notation

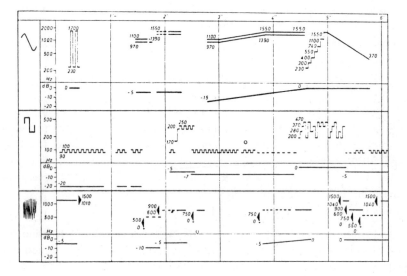

---

*Universal Edition, Vienna.

overtones in octave relationships to the fundamental. The bottom symbol represents white noise. The pitch and dynamic level of all sounds are represented graphically. Numbers in the top part of each section are the frequencies and thus fix the pitch, which in the case of noise fills a designated band. Numbers in the lower part of each section are VU meter readings which establish relative dynamic levels in decibels. Numbers across the top of the score give elapsed time in seconds.

Lejaren Hiller and Leonard Isaacson applied electronic technology to the creation of music in a very different way. Exploiting the fact that composition involves a series of choices governed by principles of organization which can be codified, they programmed selected compositional principles for an Illiac automatic high-speed digital computer. The computer generates random numbers which are interpreted as random notes. It then applies the principles of selection which have been programmed into it and produces music. Hiller and Isaacson report their computer music research in *Experimental Music*°. The book also contains the full score in conventional notation of the *Illiac Suite for String Quartet* composed by the Illiac computer.

Ultimate applications of electronic techniques to music are not in sight. They probably will have been reached when a work composed by an Illiac computer, performed by an RCA tone synthesizer, picked up by a microphone, recorded on tape, and played back through a speaker is reviewed by an electronic robot for other robots who did not make it to the concert.

System and Chance Music

Two divergent trends are apparent in recent music. One is moving toward the systematic control and total organization of musical elements according to preconceived rational procedures. The other invokes the vagaries of chance, random selection, and improvisation in the spontaneous and uninhibited creation of music. While superficially contradictory, these approaches to composition are not mutually exclusive, and some composers are active in both arenas.

The total organization concept is an outgrowth of the twelve-tone method, but where only the pitches are governed by serial order in the "classical" twelve-tone system, the new serialism extends to other parameters (a term recently appropriated from mathematics) of music such as rhythm, dynamics, articulation, density, and spacing. Olivier Messiaen and Anton Webern established precedents for the new systems, but Pierre Boulez and Karlheinz Stockhausen have far outstripped their men-

---

°New York: McGraw-Hill Book Company, Inc., 1959.

tors in bringing the elements of music under total control. Ernst Krenek is an active composer and lucid apologist for totally organized music. His article "Extents and Limits of Serial Techniques" in *The Musical Quarterly*° describes the serial procedures in several recent works.

The serialization of rhythm is too new to be standardized, but one method is this: A short time value such as a sixteenth or a thirty-second is adopted as a basic unit. This unit is numbered "1", and multiples of it up to the total in the series—12 if the rhythm series corresponds with the pitch series—are numbered consecutively. The rhythmic values thus obtained may be associated with specific notes of the pitch series, as they are in Boulez's *Structures*°° for two pianos, or they may be arranged in an arbitrary order like the notes of the pitch series.

Dynamic markings, articulation symbols, and timbre may be serialized in much the same way as rhythm. Each is arranged in a fixed order which cycles in a prescribed fashion.

Along with the serial control of additional elements has come a more sophisticated serialization of pitch than was ever envisaged by Schoenberg. Octave disposition, spacing, and texture which are free in the classic twelve-tone system have been subjected to serial regulation. Various rotational schemes have been applied to the pitch series to bring more extended sequences of notes than the twelve of the original series under direct, predetermined control. Isolated works employing these most recent and advanced techniques are just now appearing, so it is too early for meaningful deductions regarding them.

The degree of complexity concomitant with total serial organization tends to make performance by conventional means impractical, but electronic sound sources and tape recorders are equal to the task. They can execute any combination of serial procedures infallibly. As in the past the creative imagination of composers is stimulating the invention and perfection of performing mediums, and the availability of these mediums is in turn stimulating the imagination of composers.

Predetermined system would seem to be the antithesis of uncontrolled chance, but in the organization of tones the existence of common ground between them can be demonstrated. When a predetermined series of pitches is systematically associated with a predetermined series of rhythmic values, it is inevitable that a certain note in the pitch series will coincide with a certain value in the rhythm series. In one sense the value of the specific note is determined as soon as the two series are coordinated, but in another sense the value of the note is the product of a

---

°Vol. XLVI, No. 2, 1960.
°°Universal Edition, Vienna.

chance junction of the two series. The composer does not predetermine the value of the note directly though he does prescribe the procedures which produce it. In mixing sounds on tape, every element may be predetermined and rigidly controlled, but the composite sound at any instant is the product of chance association. It is a case of everything being controlled except the result, or to use Krenek's terminology, "premeditated, but unpredictable."

Music produced by computers has the same ambivalency. The machine makes selections strictly in accordance with a predetermined program, but it imposes the limits of its programmed instructions on possibilities generated by random methods.

Random selection, chance, and improvisation probably would be viewed as reactions against total control if the two trends had emerged sequentially instead of simultaneously. Since they dawned on the musical horizon in the same period, some other explanation will have to be found by musicologists of the future looking back at our time.

Random selection and chance operate in various ways. They may function as a work is being conceived or when it is being performed. John Cage, a leading exponent of chance music, exploits both possibilities. Imperfections in the paper upon which they are written determine the location of the notes in many of his compositions. Chance operations derived from *I-Ching, the Chinese Book of Changes,* are involved in the compositional process of others. His notation is usually bizarre and often subject to a variety of interpretations. His *Music for Piano 1** is written entirely in whole notes of indeterminate duration. The pianist performing Cage's *Concert for Piano and Orchestra** is free to play in any order partial or complete elements selected from the 84 different kinds of composition included in the solo part. Various materials, templates, transparencies, and written instructions provided a basis for preparing performance parts of other compositions by the players. Some scores are nothing more than directions for making a tape composition. His *Imaginary Landscape No. 4** is performed by 24 players manipulating the tuning and volume dials of 12 radios under the direction of a conductor. What comes out of the speakers is an utterly unpredictable sampling of the air waves at a particular time and place. The annotated catalog of his compositions* is a remarkable compendium of imaginative chance procedures. In this area of musical endeavor, Cage has no serious competition.

Ensemble improvisation as it is practiced by Lukas Foss and the Improvisation Chamber Ensemble (Lukas Foss, piano; Richard Dufallo, clarinet; Charles DeLancey, percussion; Howard Colf, cello) contains elements of both system and chance. It has the advantage of traditional

---

*C. F. Peters Corporation, New York.

precedents though it differs significantly from the solo and jazz improvisation which preceded it. The cooperative nature of ensemble improvisation creates problems unknown to the solo improvisor, and the rigid structural and harmonic foundations of jazz improvisation are foreign to this style of ensemble improvisation. The premises upon which it is based have not yet assumed definitive form, but currently the essential elements of a musical concept are charted using symbols peculiar to the idiom, letters, and numbers. Except to show motives or predetermined note patterns, conventional notation is not used. As the players translate the symbols into sounds, they listen critically and strive to contribute appropriate pitches, rhythms, dynamic levels, phrasing, and articulations. The element of chance is not eliminated, but it is controlled. There is a carefully calculated basis for the improvisation, and the artistic judgment of the players is consciously invoked.

Example 301 is the complete chart of *Music for Clarinet, Percussion and Piano*. The short motive is the one heard in the realization of this

Ex. 301 Music for Clarinet, Percussion and Piano

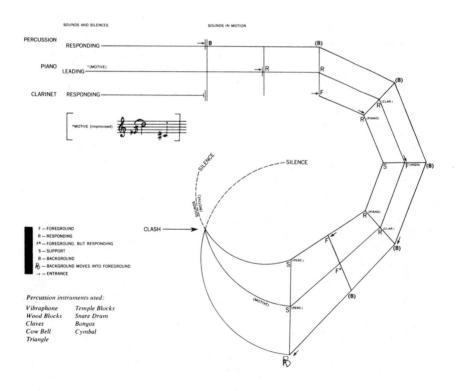

chart on RCA Vistor recordings LM-2558 and LSC-2558. It varies with each playing as does the duration of the piece. The"Sounds and Silences" section is introductory. The body of the work begins with "Sounds in Motion." Since the work is atonal, no pitches are predetermined.

These are musical experiments and innovations of the present. Which of them, if any, will dominate the music of the future? Which will fade into oblivion? Only time will tell, but every composer, performer, and listener contributes to the ultimate decision by accepting some and rejecting others.

Suggested Assignments

Extensive listening to music employing the revolutionary resources and practices discussed in this chapter is advocated rather than analysis and synthesis. Examples are listed for each category. Recordings are identified when only one is available.

1. Microtones

   Bartok: *Violin Concerto* (1938). (Quarter tones near end of first movement)

   Haba: *Fantasie for Violin Solo, Op. 9A* (1921). Folkways FM-3355

   Partch: The Bewitched (1955). Gate 5 Records Issue E. (Available only from Gate 5 Records, 1110 West Washington Boulevard, Venice, California 90291.)

   The Sound Phenomenon of Quarter-tone Music. Mesurgia A-8.

2. Rhythmic Reading and Sprechstimme

   Schoenberg, *Pierrot Lunaire, Op. 21* (1912)

   Stravinsky: *L'Histoire du Soldat* (1918)

3. Electronic Music

   Highlights of Vortex. Folkways FX- 6301

   Luening-Ussachevsky: *Poem in Cycles & Bells* (1954). Composers Recordings, Inc. CRI-112

   Sounds of New Music (1958). Folkways FX-6160

   The Sounds of Music of the RCA Electronic Music Synthesizer. RCA Victor LM-1922

   Varese: *Poeme Electronique* (1958). Columbia ML-5478; MS-6146

4. System and Chance Music

   Cage: *Indeterminacy* (1959). 2-Folkways FT-3704

   (Foss et al.): *Studies in Improvisation* (1961). RCA Victor LM-2558; LSC-2558

   Krenek: *Sestina* (1957). Epic LC-3509

CHAPTER **XVI**

Digest of Forms

The study of musical form has ample content for extensive independent courses, and frequently it is coupled with analysis or appreciation rather than composition. However, the study of composition would not be complete without some consideration of the ways resources in sonority, line, and rhythm are organized into complete works. The following digest is intended as an introduction, a review, or a supplement—depending upon individual circumstances—with some contemporary applications.

In matters of form, like most other aspects of technique, contemporary music borrows heavily from the past. Compositions which bear no resemblance to a traditional form are rare. This makes an understanding of conventional forms a logical point of departure for the study of structure in recent music and a prerequisite for composing extended works. Contemporary compositions, for the most part, are cast in the mold of some earlier form, modified to a greater or lesser degree. Since each work has its own peculiar modifications, twentieth century structures generally are more readily compared with conventional forms than with each other, though obviously many have points in common.

The fact that patterns in musical statement from previous eras persist to the present time is not an indication of arbitrary limitation or an evidence of lack of imagination. Radically new ideas have been proposed and tried, but on the whole without any real success. For instance, Alois Haba has written music in which repetition of any sort was consciously avoided. This is a revolutionary concept, but it has found little favor with listeners or other composers. Repetition is the foundation of musical form. The study of form in essence is the study of patterns of repetition.

Granting that structure in music is achieved through repetition, the possible patterns are determined by the number of thematic elements. Any given number of themes can be arranged in only so many ways, and for practical reasons the thematic material in a composition must be restricted to the amount a listener can be expected to remember. Otherwise the repetition has no meaning. A lack of alternatives accounts in part for the perennial occurrence of certain patterns over extended periods of music history.

Another reason for the prevalence of a few fundamental forms is that artistic and aesthetic considerations make some sequences of ideas more desirable than others. In the absence of objective standards, the composer may rely upon tradition and intuition in determining the sequence of his ideas, but he can no more ignore considerations of structure when organizing patterns of sound in time than an architect can ignore the force of gravity when organizing patterns of building material in space. The analogy also is made between logical sequences of musical ideas and syntax in language. Both analogies have validity. Limitations imposed on composers by the requirements of form are accepted in the interest of comprehensibility. They are no more restricting than the requirements of syntax on a novelist or a poet, and they are just as necessary.

The impression must be avoided that musical form is like a container which only has to be filled with notes to make a composition. Within the framework of a comparatively small number of basic shapes, infinite variation is possible. In a very real sense, each set of thematic ideas creates its own form. Though most compositions may be classified in a few categories, and those in each category may have many elements in common, no two are identical. Therein lies the charm and the challenge of musical form, both from the standpoint of analysis and of creation.

Part Forms

The simplest musical form consists of a single musical idea. It is characterized by a high degree of unity since contrasting ideas are lacking. It has but one complete cadence which concludes the piece. The idea may be repeated, literally or varied. Many folk and familiar songs and hymns have a one part melody which is repeated with each verse of the text. The length of individual musical ideas varies considerably, but pieces with only one are limited in extent. Contemporary composers use one part forms mostly in folk song settings and teaching pieces. Internal structures of contemporary musical periods (also called sentences), which are similar to one part forms, are illustrated in Chapter

II. Though these examples are taken from larger works, they illustrate the usual internal structures of single ideas. Observe that repeated elements often occur within a period.

Forms are extended by a cumulative process. After the one part form is a two part or *binary* form. This is the form traditional for movements of baroque suites and partitas. In these works the first part starts in the tonic key and modulates to a related key, most often the dominant, where it cadences. The second part starts in the related key, modulates back to and ends in the tonic key. Each part is repeated, so the complete form is represented schematically by the letters AA BB. The two parts may be approximately the same length, or the second may be longer. The same thematic material is used in both, but it may be modified by inversion and similar devices. The change of tonality is the main source of variety. Unifying elements are stressed, and consistency of style, tempo, and mood is maintained.

Perhaps because only limited contrast is logically possible in the two part format, three part or *ternary* designs have been in greater favor since the baroque. Essentially a ternary form consists of a statement of a thematic idea, a departure, and a return. The form is represented schematically by the letters A B A. Within this basic framework, infinite variety is possible.

The A period may be all in one key, modulate and return, or modulate and cadence in the new key. The B section may be just a bridge passage between A and its return, or it may be a phrase, a period, a group of phrases, or a developmental section based on A material. Some degree of contrast is essential, and a change of tonality is expected. The return of A may be literal, modified, abridged, or extended. If the statement cadenced in a key other than tonic, the return is altered to end in the tonic key.

The parts of ternary forms frequently are repeated. The repetition of the first part only produces the AA B A pattern typical of popular songs. Classic and romantic ternary forms often have a pattern of repetition which stems from the binary concept. The first part is repeated, and the second and third parts are repeated together, AA BA BA. Other patterns of repetition are comparatively rare. Contemporary composers are inclined to eliminate or modify repetitions. Examples of ternary form abound in all styles as short, independent pieces and as parts of larger works.

Ternary forms sometimes conclude with a *coda*. A coda is a passage beyond the basic design of the form which normally follows a cadence, real or implied, in the main tonality. A coda serves to bring the piece to a more complete and satisfying close. Codas are proportioned to the rest of the work. Those attached to simple ternary forms are brief, but it is not uncommon for larger forms to have extended, multisectional, developmental codas.

Binary and ternary forms are combined to make more extended compositions. The usual *march form* is a large binary or *compound binary* with the march proper as the first part and the trio as the second part. The march and the trio individually have simple binary or ternary structures with the usual repetitions. The trio begins and ends in a related key, usually the subdominant. Since the trio concludes the work there is no return to the tonic key. March form is the only one which regularly ends in a different key than it begins.

Marches and most other forms may begin with an *introduction*. An introduction is any passage which precedes the main body of the composition. Introductions establish the tonality and mood of the piece and set the stage for the entry of the main thematic material. They range in length and importance from a few beats of accompaniment figure to extended passages with thematic significance.

Except for marches, a far more common form is large or *compound ternary*. This is the form used for minuets, scherzos, and da capo arias. *Minuet and trio* form is another name for it. It consists of three parts of which the third is a repetition of the first. Each part is in itself a small form, usually ternary. Typically the third part is a literal return of the first, minus repeats, indicated by a *da capo* at the end of the second part. Since repeat signs are ignored in the da capo, the third part is of shorter duration than the first. In current composition extended literal repetitions are so rare, the da capo sign has all but disappeared from musical notation. Codas are fairly common in compound ternary forms, but introductions are rare.

A similar form with two trios separated by an additional return of the opening material is also encountered occasionally.

Rondo Forms

The principle of alternation is embodied in *rondo* forms. A fixed thematic element usually called a *rondo theme* alternates with subsidiary thematic elements. These subsidiary thematic elements are referred to variously as *subordinate themes, episodes,* or *digressions.* As in so many aspects of music, there is no common terminology. There is not even complete agreement on what constitutes a rondo.

The early examples have many parts each a period in length with little or no transitional material between them. The rondo theme is always in the tonic key with its appearances separated by contrasting sections in different keys. The *Gavotte en Rondeau* from Bach's *E Major Partita* for solo violin is a well known example of this type. It has nine parts with an A B A C A D A E A design.

Subsequent applications of the rondo principle have tended to reduce the number of parts to five or seven and to increase their size. Individual parts may be binary or ternary as well as one part forms. Transitional material and modulatory passages introduced between themes of rondo forms give them a degree of continuity and unity which distinguishes them from the sectional part forms. Stressing continuity, unity, and the use of transitions as decisive characteristics, some theorists classify large A B A designs which have them as rondos. Whether this form, which is common for slow movements, is more properly classified as a rondo or as a large ternary is an academic question.

The rondo principle of thematic alternation becomes apparent when three appearances of the rondo theme are separated by two contrasting sections in an A B A C A pattern. Each section may be a one part, binary, or ternary form. Transitions between sections are typical as is a coda after the third appearance of the rondo theme.

The most prevalent rondo form is achieved by bringing back the first contrasting section transposed to tonic and an additional return of the rondo theme beyond the five part plan outlined above. This gives an A B A C A B'.A design. The transposition of a subsidiary theme to the tonic key relates this type of rondo form to sonata form. When the C section is developmental, as it sometimes is, rather than a new theme, the relationship is even closer. Rondos with seven parts are inclined toward a three part balance, ABA C AB'A, with the middle part C longer than the other individual parts. The C section usually is a multipart form extended by repetitions or a multisectional development of previously stated themes.

To avoid monotony the rondo theme is modified and/or abbreviated in some of its appearances. One may even be missing. The final return of the rondo theme is the one most often omitted, and this requirement of the form is then satisfied by references to the theme in the coda. In other words, the final statement of the rondo theme is merged with the coda. The coda then is apt to be an elaborate developmental section, sometimes with references to other thematic elements as well as to the rondo theme. Mozart modified a basic seven part rondo design by suppressing the usual statement of the rondo theme between the C and B' sections, thus ABA C —B'A. In modifications such as these contemporary composers have been particularly imaginative.

The themes of rondo forms do not have to bear the weight of a development section except in the one hybrid type. The rondo and subsidiary themes typically have a straightforward songlike or dancelike quality. Between the main structural units of a rondo almost anything is possible. The close of one section may be followed immediately by the beginning of the next. More often a transition intervenes. The transition may be a simple modulatory passage which takes the most direct route to the required tonality, or it may rival the themes in extent and substance. A cohesive structure is achieved by building the transitions out of thematic material, but composers sometimes prefer to provide performers with brilliant passage work for technical display at these points.

Rondo form is used some for independent pieces but even more for finales of symphonies, sonatas, concertos, and comparable works.

Sonata Form

The tripartite concept is extended to major proportions in *sonata* form. The exposition, development, and recapitulation are three main structural divisions of approximately equal length. The material of the exposition returns with codified modifications in the recapitulation.

An introduction frequently precedes the exposition proper. It may be merely a brief passage leading to the announcement of the first theme, or it may have an extensive sectional structure. It may introduce elements of thematic significance, foreshadow future themes, or be an independent section without thematic relationship to the rest of the movement. A contrasting slow tempo normally sets the introduction apart from the exposition of fast movements in sonata form. Slow movements in the form rarely have introductions.

The exposition presents all of the thematic material, customarily with three divisions designated principal theme, subordinate theme, and closing group or first theme, second theme, and third theme. Each theme may vary in length and structure from one period to several parts depending upon the scope of the movement. The principal theme is stated entirely in the tonic in tonal compositions. The statement presents the elements of the theme in a concise fashion. Good sonata themes contain motives which are available for future development, but most of the elaboration is reserved for the development section and the coda. Contrast between the themes is essential to the modern concept of sonata form. The means of achieving the contrast, whether by changes in tonality, mood, tempo, or style varies with the period, the composer, and the work. The first theme is usually the more dramatic and energetic of the three, though exceptions occur.

The statement of the principal theme is followed by a passage of varying length and importance which leads to the mood, tempo, and tonality of the second or subordinate theme.

In tonal works the subordinate theme is in a related key, usually the dominant or relative major or minor. Contemporary examples of the form favor more remote relationships. In styles where tonality is obscure, other contrasting factors compensate. Traditionally the second theme is lyric in quality, contrasting with the first.

In early examples of the form the third or closing theme is little more than a cadential passage. Later it assumes full thematic stature, often with several distinctive motives some of which may be derived from previous themes. Fragmentary treatment is more likely in the closing section than in the statements of the first and second themes. The closing theme, which originally grew out of the second, may continue in the same tonality and mood of the preceding section, but the trend is toward greater individuality and autonomy.

The closing theme completes the exposition with a definite cadence in a tonality other than the tonic. In classic sonata forms the exposition is repeated. The double bar appearing in some contemporary works at this point is a vestigial remainder of the repeat sign. The repeat sign, where it occurs, is often ignored in current performances. Reflecting the disdain with which literal repetition is regarded, twentieth century composers practically never write it.

The skill and imagination of the composer are unfettered in the development section. Every manipulation and combination of any and all themes is invited. The introduction of new material does not violate the concept of the form, though it is superfluous when the themes have been well selected and constructed. The structure of the development is sectional. It builds up to one of the main climaxes of the movement and usually has other, secondary climax points. Remote tonalities are explored even in classic compositions. Only the tonic, which would anticipate the recapitulation, is avoided. The development may end and the principal theme make its re-entrance with a climax, or the climax in the development may subside prior to a quiet return of the first theme.

The beginning of the recapitulation is heralded by the return to the tonic tonality and an easily recognized version of the principal theme. Early users of the form were content to make the recapitulation virtually a repetition of the exposition with only the necessary changes in the transitions and the required transposition of the subordinate and closing themes. All the themes are in the tonic in the recapitulation. Departures from this tonality, if any, come between themes. The problem of avoiding monotony while bringing back all the themes in one key long has occupied composers, and many solutions have been found. Twentieth century sonata forms, in which tonality is less decisive as a structural element, achieve unity and variety with other means, and typical freedom of tonality is exercised in the recapitulation as elsewhere.

The recapitulation completes the basic sonata form, but more often than not it is followed by a coda. The coda may be no more than a brief cadential passage which serves to bring the movement to a close, but it may have an extended sectional structure and amount practically to a second development section. The coda may use material from any of the themes and introduce new ideas as well. The recall of elements from the introduction is an effective unifying device. Extended codas frequently have the biggest climax of the movement, but they also may lead to quiet endings. Finding just the right conclusion for a movement is one of the arts of composition.

Quite a few early examples of sonata form indicate a repetition of the development and recapitulation together. This reflects the pattern of repetition associated with simple ternary form in which the first part is repeated and the second and third parts repeated together. Conductors and performers hardly ever observe repeat signs at the end of a movement in sonata form, and composers have long since ceased to write them. That the same pattern of repetition exists at all in simple ternary and extended sonata forms is an indication of the underlying relationship between them.

The foregoing summarizes the general characteristics of sonata form. An examination of specific works will reveal infinite variation of detail within this broad outline.

Sonata form, with its ternary implication, has a binary counterpart —*abridged sonata* or *sonatina* form. This form has all the features of sonata form except the development. The exposition is followed immediately or after a bridge passage by the recapitulation. In the absence of a development section the coda sometimes assumes added importance and in a sense becomes a development section though it retains its position following the recapitulation.

A modified sonata form with a double exposition is customary for first movements of concertos. The first exposition in the orchestra is all in the tonic key. The solo participates in the second exposition which has the usual sonata form key relationships. A cadenza comes after a tonic six-four chord in the tonic key between the recapitulation and the coda.

The form diagramed in the section on rondo forms exhibiting certain sonata form characteristics (ABA C AB'A) is a sort of hybrid. Generally classified as rondos, these hybrids are variously known as *rondo-sonatas, sonata-rondos,* or simply as a type of rondo. They have alternate repetitions of a theme, like rondo forms, and a return of the second theme transposed to the tonic key, like sonata forms. The fourth of their seven parts may be a new theme or a development section. Those with a new theme are more akin to rondo form; those with a development section are closer to sonata form.

Contrapuntal Forms

The forms previously considered sometimes are lumped together as homophonic forms as distinguished from the contrapuntal forms. The fundamental difference stems from the manner of repetition. Homophonic forms are achieved by alternate repetition, that is, the reappearance of themes after a departure, while the contrapuntal forms are achieved primarily by immediate repetition in another voice.

Repetition in a *canon* is continuous. A line started in one part is imitated a few beats or measures later in one or more other parts. The imitation may be at the unison or any interval. The end of *round canons* or *rounds* leads back to the beginning, so they can be repeated ad infinitum. Others break the imitation at the end to make a cadence. Canons with the imitation in inversion, retrograde, retrograde inversion, augmentation, and diminution are possible. Canons may be accompanied by free voices.

Despite some notable exceptions, the strict imitation of the canon limits its usefulness as an independent form. Its principal function is in passages of works with some other overall structure.

Fugue, on the other hand, is a form admirably suited to complete works in a wide variety of styles. It starts with the statement of a concise theme, called a *subject,* in one voice alone. The subject is then stated in succession by each of the other voices of the fugue, most often three or four. As each completes its statement of the subject, it continues with a counterpoint to the subsequent subject appearance. When one counterpoint is systematically associated with the subject, it assumes thematic significance and is known as a *countersubject.* The main exposition of the fugue is complete when each voice has stated the subject. Sometimes there is an extra subject entrance in the exposition or a counter exposition, in which each voice has the subject a second time.

Traditionally, the second voice states the subject a fifth above or a fourth below the first. This version is called the *answer.* It is *real* if the intervals are identical with the subject; *tonal* if they are altered to preserve the tonality of the subject. Modern composers favor real answers, and answers at intervals other than the fourth and fifth are common.

The main exposition is followed by a series of entrances of the subject in various voices and keys. In this section all sorts of manipulations and combinations of the subject and countersubject are exploited. Passages of free counterpoint, usually employing motives from the subject or countersubject, intervene between thematic entrances.

The return to the tonic key characteristically is associated with an overlapping or *stretto* of subject entrances which concludes the form.

Fugal expositions and fuguelike passages called *fugatos* frequently are incorporated in other forms, especially in the development sections of sonata forms.

Variation Forms

The variation principle consists of the continuous repetition of one or more thematic elements while the others are varied. Historically, variations are classified according to the particular element repeated.

Chorale preludes, which are a type of variation, use the chorale melody as the basis of the variations. The melody is embellished, provided with enriched settings, or its phrases used imitatively in the variations.

Chaconnes and *passacaglias* use a bass line or a harmonic progression as the fixed element. The bass theme or progression, which has period structure, is repeated without interruption through the variations. *Grounds* and *ostinatos* illustrate similar procedures with a shorter repeated element.

Classic variations usually have a theme in binary or ternary form, frequently with repetitions. The melody of the theme and the harmonies which accompany it may serve as the basis for variations, and the original structure of the theme with any distinctive modulations and cadences is retained. Since the closed form of the theme ends with a full cadence, each variation does also. This produces a break between variations and a sectional structure which contrasts with the continuous flow of the type exemplified by the passacaglia and chaconne.

Free variations are a more recent type. In free variations a theme is used as a point of departure, but beyond that no procedures are prescribed. A motive may be extracted from the theme to provide the only thematic reference in an entire variation. The melodic, harmonic, and rhythmic material may be new and the form of individual variations different from each other and from the theme. When all of the elements are subject to variation, careful analysis is sometimes necessary to reveal the tenuous relationship between the theme and the variations. The variation techniques employed in free variations are not peculiar to the variation forms. They are found in the developmental passages of all forms.

Sectional variations do not lend themselves to the building of monumental climaxes. When required this function is served by a finale which deserts the pattern of the preceding variations in favor of a more climactic procedure such as that of a fugue.

The unity implicit in the variation concept appeals to contemporary composers, and at least residual traces of all variation types exist in twentieth century music.

Multimovement Forms

Individual forms are combined in multimovement forms. Pairs of dances were joined at an early date. These were forerunners of the baroque *suites* and *partitas* which consisted of a group of dance movements in contrasting tempos and styles. The choice and sequence of movements was not completely standardized, but the most prevalent arrangement had an *allemande, courante, sarabande,* and *gigue* in that order. An optional group was often inserted between the sarabande and the gigue, and variously titled preludes sometimes preceded the allemandes. The movements were usually in the same key, but the opposite mode both parallel and relative was sometimes used. Twentieth century dance suites, of which there are many, are direct descendants of the dance pairs and baroque suites, though none of the earlier conventions are still observed.

Serenade, cassation, and *divertimento* are multimovement types which flourished during the classic era. All three terms are applied to multimovement works for various instrumental combinations. Beyond this, little in the way of uniform criteria can be detected in the various examples of these forms. They are the models followed by the modern suites comprised of assorted movements which do not conform to any pre-existent plan. The movements for such suites are often taken from dramatic works—ballets, operas, and motion picture scores. Suites excerpted from dramatic works make appropriate sections of the complete composition available for concert performances.

Unlike suites, which may have any number of movements in random order, *complete sonatas* adhere to uniform standards firmly established by tradition. Symphonies, sonatas, trios, quartets, and all similar works are cast in complete sonata form. Only the mediums are different.

The classic complete sonata form consists of four movements. The first is in sonata form and has a fast tempo. The second is a slow movement. Broad ternary, sonata, and variation forms are common. The third movement originally was a minuet-trio-minuet, but starting with Beethoven a scherzo frequently replaces the minuet. The fourth movement is a sonata or rondo form in a fast tempo. When the first movement is only moderately fast, the order of the second and third movements is sometimes reversed.

From a standpoint of tonality, the first, third, and fourth movements normally are in the tonic key. The second (slow) movement is in a related tonality, most often the subdominant. Exceptions occurred almost from the beginning, and even token compliance vanished before the present century.

No thematic relationship between movements is anticipated, but from Beethoven on common elements have been incorporated in different movements as an added unifying device. A cyclic form results when this is done systematically.

Concertos typically have three movements corresponding to the first, second, and fourth of a symphony. This same plan of movements is not uncommon in other mediums. The second and third movements of concertos sometimes are played without interruption. This practice, too, appears in other types of composition.

Vocal Forms

Form in vocal music is achieved in the same manner as in instrumental music, i.e., by various patterns of repetition, and most if not all of the instrumental forms have counterparts in vocal music. Simple binary and ternary are adaptable to setting many texts, and these forms are sometimes known as *song forms*. The minuet and trio form and the da capo aria form have much in common. The earliest known canons and rounds are for voices, and the contrapuntal forms are equally effective for voices or instruments. Vocal pieces in sonata form and the larger rondo forms are possible but not usual. In addition, two types of songs—*strophic* and *through-composed*—have forms peculiar to vocal music.

A strophic song is one in which the same music is used for all the verses of a poem. This type of setting is appropriate only for poems with uniform stanzas and a relatively constant mood. It is usual in folk and children songs and is found in many art songs as well.

The antithesis of a strophic setting is a through-composed setting. In through-composition the text dictates the music at each instant, and there is no systematic repetition. This does not preclude the use of unifying devices such as motives and accompaniment figures, but they are subservient to the text. On a larger scale, operas and oratorios are through-composed in the sense that the sequence of musical events is determined largely by the plot and the text, though internal sections may fit in familiar patterns. One purpose of *leitmotivs* is to provide a unifying device independent of sectional repetitions.

Each text presents special problems in form and suggests unique solutions. For this reason structural stereotypes in vocal music result mostly from bending texts (by way of spurious repetitions) to comply with preconceived abstract patterns such as that of the da capo aria. The former proclivity of composers for instrumental forms in vocal music was perhaps the result of conditioning. In contemporary vocal writing as a rule the form springs from the text, and the literary and musical ideas shape the form rather than vice versa. Ideally, each work both vocal and instrumental creates its own form.

Program and Dramatic Music

Program music is out of vogue at the present time and merits little space in a book on contemporary composition. This is an age of absolute music and a strong return to classic concepts of form. Program music stands in the same relation to its program as vocal music does to its text. Literary or pictorial considerations may be decisive in the form, but the influence of purely musical factors is not automatically excluded in programmatic works. The most successful program pieces seem to be those which have a satisfying abstract musical form and merely offer listeners a programmatic association as an added inducement.

Generalities about the form of music written to accompany dances, plays, and films are futile, because each composition is unique. Composers with a good command of abstract musical organization are equipped to satisfy the structural requirements of dramatic music, which on the whole are less demanding because of the added visual aspect of the production. Listeners are rarely concerned about the musical form of dramatic pieces, because their attention is focused on, or one could say distracted by, the other elements.

Contemporary Adaptations

The endurance of traditional musical forms through changing periods and styles attests to their adaptability and their validity. The concepts embodied in traditional forms, adjusted to current resources and requirements, persist to the present time. Certain trends are evident as conventional forms are tailored to contemporary taste.

The role of tonality has changed radically in recent times. Once a dominant unifying force and source of variety, its influence has diminished with the adoption of broader concepts of tonality. Music with obvious tonal centers achieves variety by modulation and unity by returning to the original key. The effectiveness of this procedure is reduced when the tonality is vague or ambiguous, and it ceases to exist when atonality is approached. For composers currently working with well defined tonalities, tonality functions as always, but remote tonal relationships are exploited both for their own sake and as features of the structure.

Reflecting no doubt the rush of modern living, contemporary composers present their ideas tersely. Brevity is venerated. It is achieved not by reducing the content but by eliminating the unessential and tautological. Literal repetitions are scarce, and extended modulatory transitions are unnecessary when abrupt shifts in tonality are commonplace. The succinct succession of ideas requires the concentrated attention of listeners, and composers operate on the premise that attentive listening will prevail. That their optimism is not always justified has not yet led to widespread compromise on this issue.

A high degree of coherence is typical of twentieth century composition. The exploitation of brief, flexible motives, often with a prominent rhythmic element, contributes substantially to logical integration. Freedom in forming vertical and linear associations and revived emphasis on contrapuntal procedures facilitates the manipulation of motives.

One modification of standard forms has been used sufficiently to achieve independent status and have a name—*arch form*. It results from reversing the order of the themes in the recapitulation of sonata forms. This form is represented schematically by the letters A B C D C B A, with A, B, and C as the thematic elements and D as the development section. Sometimes only the order of the first and second themes is reversed, and the principle is applicable with fewer parts, A B C B A. The middle section may be new material, and it probably will be in five part arch forms. It should be noted that an A B A form exhibits on a small scale the mirroring of themes on either side of a central point characteristic of arch forms. Bartok was a leading exponent of arch form.

The meaning of the term *symphony* has been extended to include vocal compositions and works for orchestra satisfying few of the conditions of the classic form. Of particular interest are symphonies in one movement. Examples from three, by Sibelius, Schuman, and Harris, are quoted in previous chapters. There are not yet enough of them to produce a standardized pattern, but they are spawned by the urge to create a more highly unified symphonic work of major proportions than is attainable with the conventional multimovement structure—the same motivating force which led to cyclic symphonies. The one movement symphony appears as a twentieth century solution to a perennial problem. In a one movement symphony the elements of three or four movements may be compressed into a single movement, or the proportions of a single sonata form may be augmented to become a full symphony.

Probably the greatest innovation in musical form is the twelve-tone technique. Twelve-tone music can be written in any form, but the series itself is a structural element. The series has been proposed as a substitute in atonal music for tonality. Little else has been suggested to fill the void created by the disintegration of tonality. Some musicians deny the possibility of any suitable substitute for tonality, but others equally firm in their convictions regard serial procedures as the ideal solution to this and several other problems of modern music. Each composer decides for himself which path to follow.

The various forms of the series provide opportunities for systematic arrangements. For example, Krenek in his *Twelve Short Piano Pieces*° uses the different forms of the series according to the following scheme:

1. O
2. I
3. R
4. RI
5. O and I
6. O and R
7. O and RI
8. I and R
9. I and RI
10. O, R, and RI
11. O, I, and R
12. O, I, R, and RI

The four forms of the series and their transpositions have unlimited possibilities for schematic arrangements of this sort. They may serve as the exclusive structural element or be used in conjunction with conventional formal devices.

°G. Schirmer, Inc., 1939.

This sums up the structural patterns which have been most useful to composers of the past and present. Familiarity with them is essential, but knowing them and using them is no guarantee of successful organization. Conceiving the form of a composition is as much a part of the creative process as conceiving the themes. Just as no two themes are identical, no two forms are identical. The form and the themes are dependent upon each other for full realization of their potentials. The composer's quest is for an ideal shape with ideal content.

Suggested Assignments

Assignments exclusively in analysis are omitted in the expectation that this area will have been covered elsewhere. If previous training in form has not included contemporary examples, analysis of recent music is highly recommended. Bartok's *Mikrokosmos** has many examples of small, but not necessarily simple, structures. His string quartets are models of terse organization, with movements and even complete quartets growing out of a few concise motives. Hindemith's *Ludus Tonalis*** contains a dozen fugues worth studying as contemporary examples of the form. His symphonies, chamber music, and sonatas provide a good introduction to larger forms in a twentieth century idiom. Schoenberg provides the clearest examples of twelve-tone music.

Themes and sketches written as exercises for the previous chapters may serve as a source of thematic material for the suggested assignments below. The same theme may be used in more than one assignment if it is appropriate. The principles of form can be mastered as efficiently, if not more so, by writing the simplest possible texture, minimizing problems of sonority and counterpoint while concentrating on structure. The essential elements of form can be incorporated in a single line with occasional harmonies at critical points. Some composers habitually sketch the main outline of the complete work before filling in the details. Two solo instruments like flute and clarinet or violin and viola are good mediums for the larger forms when time or skill is limited. Two part writing for the piano can be used in the same way. Writing variations is an effective discipline for developing the techniques required to compose sonata and rondo forms.

1. Write a binary form in which the thematic elements of the first part are modified appropriately in the second part.

2. Write a ternary form in which the return of the opening material is modified for added interest.

---

*Hawkes & Son, Ltd., 1940.
**Schott & Co., Ltd., 1943.

3. Expand the ternary form to one like a minuet and trio by adding a contrasting middle part and a da capo.

4. Compose a rondo, striving for interest in the transitions and for an effective relationship between the themes.

5. Compose a sonata form. The work does not have to be long. Single periods may be used as themes, but include all of the essential elements. Delay experimental modifications until a grasp of the regular form has been demonstrated.

6. (For students who have had training in canon and fugue) Write a fugue making full use of contemporary resources.

7. Write a short set of variations of the classic type using either an original theme or one taken from another composer.

8. Select a short poem and make an appropriate setting for it. Strive for a coherent musical structure independent of the unity provided by the text.

9. (For composers attracted to the twelve-tone technique) Write a piece using a systematic arrangement of the forms of the series as the basis of organization.

CHAPTER XVII

Practical Suggestions

Young composers frequently ask whether it is better to write with a piano or without. There is no answer other than for each to discover by trial and error what works best for him, and it is not necessarily the same for every type of composing. An instrument is of little help in conceiving and notating rhythms, and frequently none is necessary in writing melodies. On the other hand, comparatively few inexperienced composers can write complex harmonic progressions infallibly without reference to the piano.

There are certain dangers in relying too heavily on an instrument. One is that it fosters the habit of improvising rather than composing, and many good ideas no doubt have been lost as a result. Another danger especially applicable to pianists is that they tend to write finger patterns rather than anything truly creative. Also, those who write with an instrument tend to dissipate valuable time playing a progression or melody over and over before writing it, and the final version may be no better than the first. Effective revision is more likely after the ideas are down in black and white.

On the other side of the ledger, interesting sonorities and idiomatic figurations have resulted from chance discoveries at the keyboard, and wrong notes and faulty progressions have been found and corrected with the aid of the piano. Whether one writes everything or nothing at the piano or uses a compromise system, again he has good company in the ranks of distinguished composers, for among them methods ranging from one extreme to the other are used successfully.

The ability to write legible music manuscript is a prime requisite for a composer. This comes with practice, and proper equipment is helpful. Black ink should be used, and a true carbon ink such as *Higgins*

Eternal and those specially prepared are best. Ordinary fountain pen inks are not sufficiently dense for duplication by the usual processes. If a fountain pen is used, *Pelikan Fount India* ink made by Günther Wagner in Hanover, Germany but available in this country is recommended. Other India inks duplicate satisfactorily but are prone to clog fountain pens.

Several companies make fountain pens for music copying. The best is a matter of individual preference. Some copyists prepare an ordinary fountain pen with an inexpensive, replaceable point for music copying by filing the point slightly to broaden it and give it the desired angle. This requires experimentation, but a point exactly suited to one's individual requirements is worth the effort. Fountain pens have two disadvantages. They are relatively heavy, a decided problem when used for extended periods, and the carbon inks deposit sediment in them unless they are cleaned thoroughly after each use.

For these reasons many copyists prefer a steel nib in a lightweight holder. They are inexpensive and easily replaced when wear or carbon deposits impair their efficiency. Their most serious limitation is that they require frequent dipping. This can be partially alleviated by using in conjunction with the nib an *inkspoon* of the type manufactured by H. Mauri & Company, New York, and available at stationers and artist suppliers. The best make and style of nib is again a matter of individual preference, but an *Esterbrook No. 442 Jackson Stub* has been found very satisfactory.

The penpoint selected must be capable of producing all the music symbols with a minimum of effort and a maximum of speed. Note heads and beams must be broad, and note stems and bar lines must be relatively thin. This means that the point must be capable of producing broad lines when drawn from left to right and narrow lines when drawn down. Many copyists insist on a point that will fill a staff space with a solid note head in one stroke. Others use a circular motion for solid note heads. Open notes are made with two strokes going in the same direction, left to right. A point fulfilling these requirements will probably taper slurs and ties properly. Large notes are easier to read, and this is important in instrumental parts, slightly less so in scores.

Notes which sound simultaneously must be exactly aligned on the score. Improper alignment is a source of difficulty in performing and analyzing manuscript music.

Frequent rehearsal numbers or letters are a requirement in orchestral and chamber music scores and parts. The complexity and unfamiliarity of contemporary works leads to much starting and stopping in rehearsals, and time is always at a premium. Having a rehearsal number every ten or twelve measures conserves valuable rehearsal time.

A common source of delay in rehearsals is incorrect parts. Preferably every note should be checked, but at least the number of measures in each part should be counted. Even the most experienced copyist occasionally will omit a measure or miscount a rest.

Multiple copies of scores and parts are frequently required. The Ozalid process is generally the most economical and satisfactory method of reproducing limited quantities. This process requires a master copy written on transparent paper, but no special problems are involved in preparing the master. Ordinary pen and ink are used, and the manuscript is written in the same manner as on opaque paper. Some composers score directly on transparent paper and avoid recopying. Typewriting will duplicate by the Ozalid process if it is done with a carbon ribbon or with carbon paper backing the transparent.

Music-lined transparent paper in various sizes and arrangements, some with clefs, is available from several manufacturers and from widespread dealers. Metropolitan areas usually have companies which specialize in music printing. In areas where specialized service is not available, blueprint and drafting companies usually can duplicate transparents. Their prints may be blueline rather than the blackline preferred by musicians, but such prints are usable.

Copies can be made from opaque paper by various processes, but the cost is higher than for copies from transparent paper. For limited quantities, a transparent master usually is made from the opaque copy, and prints then are made by the Ozalid process. For larger quantities, photo-offset printing is the most satisfactory method. The result is an excellent duplication of the original, and the cost, spread over many units, is minimal.

Ditto, mimeograph, and multilith sometimes are used for duplicating music, and though they are useful, these processes are not completely satisfactory for most requirements of the composer.

In the past few years machines similar to typewriters have been devised for copying music. They have limitations and are too expensive for the average beginning composer, but they are capable of producing music symbols comparable in appearance and legibility to those in published music. Perfected and mass produced they will be a great boon to composers and arrangers.

When a composer has a work written and copied, his next problem is in finding a performer. This is not always easy for an unestablished composer, but it is not an insurmountable difficulty. Performers and conductors are becoming more receptive to new works. High school, college, and university musical organizations are an attractive outlet. Friends and acquaintances can be induced to include new compositions on their recitals. Competitions and commissions are an added incentive for writing, and performances of sucessful works are assured. Getting performances and recognition are second in importance in a composer's career only to the composing itself.

The choice of medium and difficulty are critical factors in getting performances. Works written especially for friends, with their capabilities and limitations in mind, are certain to be appreciated. Compositions for instruments or combinations for which the literature is sparse are more apt to receive favorable reception than string quartets and symphonies. Works which take into account the technical limitations and instrumentation of amateur groups will be performed sooner and more often than those demanding professional standards. These suggestions point to solo instruments (preferably played by friends), less usual chamber music combinations, and band as the logical outlets for younger composers.

Few are optimistic enough to expect to make a living from composition, but seeing one's music in print is not too much to hope for. Though the popular music field is practically closed to outsiders, and manuscripts are returned unopened, prospects in other areas are somewhat more favorable. Publishers interested in showing a profit are not eager to bring out new works in competition with masters of the past. Their reluctance to publish contemporary string quartets and symphonies by unknown composers reflects practical considerations rather than lack of interest or merit. The most favorable area of endeavor for composers who aspire to publication is in school music. Selected lists for school music groups are comprised primarily of recent compositions and arrangements. Difficulty and style are restricted, which discourages many composers, but publishers are always interested in new works suitable for the mass market of the public schools.

Composers lament the conservative and often unimaginative idiom of much school music, but composing for this market is a tremendous challenge and opportunity. School age is not too young to expose coming generations of musicians and music lovers to the riches of the contemporary musical language. Their attitudes and taste for years to come will reflect the indoctrination they receive from their teachers, present and future.

Contemporary music is not an esoteric art intended only for the initiated. It is for everybody. Novices are easily dazzled and confused by its intricacies and complexities, but its sounds can be comprehended by everyone with the desire and the patience to listen. However rapidly music has changed in the past sixty years, its main streams still follow logical courses, and its roots are well anchored in tradition. The new sounds of our time are not fads that will disappear without a trace, but rather the culmination of the past and the foundation of the future which always meet in the present. This book will succeed in its purpose to the extent it illuminates these concepts and contributes to the understanding and command of the TECHNIQUES OF TWENTIETH CENTURY COMPOSITION.

Index of Examples

Sincere appreciation is expressed to the publishers who generously granted permission to quote from their publications. The page numbers provided with the examples refer to their location in the editions indicated. When two publishers are given, the second is the agent or distributor for the United States. Complete copyright data appears below examples which are not in the public domain. Dates for works are the approximate date of composition or of first publication.

Publisher	*Abbreviation*
Associated Music Publishers, Inc.	AMP
C. C. Birchard & Company	BIR
Boosey and Hawkes, Inc.	B&H
Boosey & Co., Ltd.	
Hawkes & Son, Ltd.	
Breitkopf and Härtel	BrH
Broadcast Music, Inc.	BMI
J. & W. Chester, Ltd.	JWC
J. Curwen & Sons, Ltd.	CUR
Durand & Cie.	DUR
Eastman School of Music	ESM
Elkan-Vogel Co.	EV
Carl Fischer, Inc.	CF
Wilhelm Hansen	WH
Harms, Inc.	HAR
Hawkes & Son, Ltd. (see Boosey and Hawkes, Inc.)	
Heugel & Cie.	HEU
International Music Company	IMC
Edwin F. Kalmus	KAL

Anonymous
The Ash Grove, 3

Barber, Samuel (1910—)
Concerto for Violin, Op. 14 (1941), reduction, GS, 49
Symphony No. 1, Op. 9 (1936), score, GS, 162

Barlow, Wayne (1912—)
Rhapsody for Oboe, *The Winter's Past* (1938), score, ESM, 88, 90

Bartok, Bela (1881-1945)
Concerto for Orchestra (1943), score, B&H, 48, 50, 51, 129, 174
Concerto No. 2 for Piano (1931), score, UE-B&H, 77, 81
Concerto No. 3 for Piano (1945), score, B&H, 56, 98, 129, 130, 146,
    171, 173, 175
Concerto for Violin (1938), score, B&H, 182, 195
Duos for Two Violins (1931), B&H, 41
For Children (1908), piano, KAL, 111
Mikrokosmos (1926-37), piano, B&H, 39, 40, 41, 76, 107, 109, 110,
    123, 126, 132, 138, 145, 149, 159, 174
Quartet No. 2 (1917), score, B&H, 122, 125, 164
Quartet No. 4 (1928), score, B&H, 164
Quartet No. 5 (1934), score, B&H, 48, 82, 109, 134, 152
Sonatina for Piano (1915), KAL, 22

Beethoven, Ludwig van (1770-1827)
Symphony No. 3 in E-flat, Op. 55 (1804), KAL, 5

Berg, Alban (1885-1935)
Concerto for Violin (1935), score, UI-AMP, 179
Wozzeck (1914-21), piano-vocal, UI-AMP, 35, 44, 79

Index